THE MATTER OF
THE
HIJACKED
ARTIFACTS

If it's worthless, why steal it?

Steve Levi

Master of the Impossible Crime

PUBLICATION
CONSULTANTS
WE BELIEVE IN THE POWER OF AUTHORS

PO Box 221974 Anchorage, Alaska 99522-1974
books@publicationconsultants.com, www.publicationconsultants.com

ISBN Number: 978-1-63747-271-2
eBook ISBN Number: 978-1-63747-272-9

Library of Congress Number: 2023941285

Manufactured in the United States of America

CHAPTER 1

Heinz Noonan, the 'Bearded Holmes' of the Sandersonville Police Department, was not particularly pleased to be in Alaska. It wasn't Alaska he was displeased with. It was his in-laws. But when you are married to an Alaskan, sooner or later, you must associate with those in-laws. Noonan was a firm believer of the famous George Burns quote "Happiness is having a large, loving, caring, close-knit family in another city."

All was going as well as could be expected. His wife was hobnobbing with high school friends, the twins were with their grandfather fishing for something, probably halibut, out of Seward, and his mother-in-law (thankfully) was at some church social. This left him alone, *suffering* (he told his wife), and free to do whatever. The *whatever* today was the Municipal Museum with its multiple floors of Native cultural icons and artifacts. The only curse, so speak, was it was July, and summer in Alaska is chockablock with tourists, most of whom only know one thing about Alaska: how to spell it.

As Noonan had learned over the years, one must be very careful when speaking to Alaskans during the summer. This is more than a regional consideration but an intellectual one as well. Alaskans, from about May 15th to June 1st, the first two weeks of tourist season, are amiable sorts. They are understanding of the wildest fantasies of tourists and answer the most ludicrous of questions with honesty. But by June

2nd, Alaskans have become tired of informing tourists the northland has no penguins, there are no two-story igloos, you cannot purchase blubber stew in any restaurant in town and while there are ice worms, they are not large enough to attack the huskies pulling sleds through the snow.

So, after June 2nd, Alaskans lie.

It's not actually *lying*.

It's called absurding.

If a tourist asks a crazy question about the northland, Alaskans take the matter one step further.

They absurd it.

As an example, if a tourist asks if American dollars will be accepted in a Native village, the Alaskan will say "Of course, but the change you get will be in ivory chips." If a tourist asks how Alaskans mow their front lawn when it is covered with snow, the Alaskan replies "Oh, we just lower the wheels." And when it comes to earthquakes, Alaskans do not have to worry about any furniture moving because "We spray water on the backs of our bureaus and press them against the ice walls in our bedroom. That way they freeze in place. And in the villages, the bureaus have rounded backs to fit snuggly against the walls of the igloos." What is most amazing is how many tourists believe what the Alaskans are absurding them.

Of all the exhibits in the Municipal Museum where Noonan was hiding out for the afternoon, the one artifact Noonan never tired of viewing was the Aleut gut-skin raincoat. This Native artifact was made of the stomach and intestine of a seal and stitched with sinew. For Noonan, this was proof there was no limit to human ingenuity. Even better, the raincoat was an excellent example that so-called primitive people were far more adept at recycling than the rest of us will ever be.

All was going well, academically speaking, until the electronic Beelzebub, the cursed tool of Satan, the anodic Lucifer, burped to life in his vest pocket. Noonan raised his eyebrows in annoyance because, after all, he was on vacation. He was supposed to be immune from calls from the home office and, considering he was in Alaska, he was a long way from any office politics in North Carolina. But then again, he was required to have the wireless demon within reach at all times by the two people who controlled his life: his wife and the Sandersonville Commissioner of Homeland Security.

It was neither.

It was an Inupiat named Oliver Atka.

Noonan knew that from the readout on the cathodic goblin.

Noonan was going to ignore to the pulsating beast when he heard a voice behind him.

"Aren't you going to answer?"

Surprised, the detective turned and saw a man, clearly a Native by his facial structure but probably part white because he was well over six feet tall.

"Sorry?"

"The phone. Aren't you going to answer my call?"

"Your call?" Noonan was clearly confused. "If you're here, why are you calling me? And, speaking of that, who are you?"

"Oliver Atka. Just as it says on your phone. Your wife said you were reluctant to answer your phone on vacation. She said you were probably at the Municipal Museum. I work here so I thought I would give you a call. To identify you. And here I am!" He spread his arms in a welcoming gesture.

Noonan looked from the phone to Atka and then back to the phone. Atka clicked his phone off and Noonan's electronic beast ceased buzzing.

"Abracadabra," Atka said as he put his phone in his dress jacket breast pocket.

"Quite an introduction," Noonan said as he slipped his Beelzebub back into his cargo pant side pocket. "OK, I'm here. What swamp did my wife toss me into?"

"Bones, Captain."

"No, Heinz. Until there's a crime, I'm Heinz."

"Heinz, fine. I'm Oliver. I am the Native Artifact Specialist and Curator here. It's all about bones. They aren't here."

"What do you mean, 'They aren't here?'"

"Short story, actually. There was a large museum here in Anchorage that closed. It does happen, you know. Museums are not forever. This one was in the National Bank of Anchorage and the bank wanted more room for whatever. So, it closed the museum, artifacts and all. Artifacts have no real value, street value that is, so they were transferred to museums across the state."

"Let me guess, like bones."

Now Atka was serious. "Yes, but it is more complicated than that. Museums are odd ducks in the business world. They have property that is so well known the items cannot be sold, like the Mona Lisa, or are only historically significant because of who owned them. Like an ivory carving of a whale. You can buy an ivory carving of a whale here in Anchorage in a lot of shops. But if the carving was done by a specific, well-known ivory carving artist, it has greater value than one by an artist no one has heard of."

Noonan leaned back against a wall in the hallway as he dug in his jacket pocket for a pen.

"Here's a notepad," Atka said as he handed Noonan a small booklet. "Your wife said you lived and died on notebook pages."

Noonan took the notebook. "So nice of her," he said flatly. He flipped to a blank page and dug a pen out of his pant pocket. "Now, following up on what you said." He paused. "About the ivory carving. The ivory carvings I've seen, the good ones, have the name of the artist on the artwork. Usually on the bottom."

"Correct. But you have to be careful. I do not know if you are aware of it, but only Natives can carve ivory. The name on the bottom of the artwork is to make it legal to sell. If a Native comes in from a village and wants to sell his ivory to a gift store, he has to show his or her name on the bottom of the carvings to the vendor. As long as the name on the bottom of the carving matches the Native's ID or his Blood Quantum Card, that's proof the work was done by a Native."

"I've heard that's the case."

"Keeps everyone within the law. Do you know what a provenance is?"

Noonan nodded. "A written record of the history of the objects. Who made it, who bought it, when. That kind of information."

"Yes. But not every object has one. That's important to understand when it comes to museum artifacts. See, when you bought that ivory whale from the gift shop, all you have is the bill of sale. You are not going to get a provenance for that whale. It was legal to sell, and if you give it away, or sell it, it's just like a piece of furniture. It was legal for you to buy and therefore legal for you to sell."

"Where is this going?"

"I'm getting to that. We were talking about artifacts with value. The valuable artifacts are the ones where a well-known artist did the work. Anyone can fake a Picasso, but without the provenance, it just pigments on canvas."

"True."

"Native artifacts are the same way. With a provenance from a well-known artist, the carved whale has a high value."

"OK. But I thought you were talking about bones."

"I was. And I am. I just wanted to make sure you understood the value of things in a museum. Human bones are the same. If you find a bone on your property, a human bone, it's best to contact the authorities. A lot of times it's from a family burial. It's legal to bury a body on your property if you follow the state guidelines. Or, in the case of Alaska, Territorial guidelines. It's not finders' keepers though. If it's an Indian bone, the law is loosey-goosey. Technically, if you find Indian bones on federal land, they are protected. On private land, once they are identified as Native bones, well, you can keep them. That's why a museum can have Native bones."

Noonan gave Atka a strange look. "I thought Native bones were being sent back to where they were found. And reburied. What am I missing?"

"I have a 'yes and no' answer."

'I hate those kinds of answers."

Atka shook his head humorously. "No, the bones do not have to be sent back. Sometimes they are, sometimes not. There is a lot of scientific information in old bones and Native bones are significantly different than, say, the bones of a white man of the same era in Scotland or Saudi Arabia. Then there is the matter of not knowing where the bones were found in the first place. In the old days, like the 1600s, there were no museums. Rich people had what were called 'cabinets of curiosities.' Rich people collected bones and artifacts and artwork and relics from their travels all over the world and displayed them in these cabinets of curiosities. A century later – after having been sold or inherited or passed around – no one knew for sure where the bones and artifacts and relics came from in the first place."

"But the bones?" Noonan let the sentence hang. "What does all of this have to do with Alaska?"

"When Alaska was bought by the United States in 1867 all Native bones found in Alaska were on federal land. For decades, any bones found were just tossed aside. Early explorers dug up the graves looking for artifacts. Sometimes the bones were reburied, other times they were just tossed aside. Animals took them. Spring floods moved them. Finding loose bones was not uncommon. Tracing them back to their roots, so to speak, was very difficult."

Noonan tapped his notebook page. "This is all well and good, but it does not tell me why we are talking about bones in the first place."

"Because the museum that went *kaput* had Native bones. They were supposed to come here for study and possible reinternment."

"OK, again, so why are we talking about bones?"

"Because the bones have disappeared. Along with the entire museum."

CHAPTER 2

Noonan stalled in his writing. "The museum disappeared?"

"Not the building. The artifacts. The contents. Bones and all."

Noonan wrote 'missing' in his notebook as he shook his head. "I see." But from the expression on his face, he didn't. "What was the size of the museum? I mean, was it like the size of a closet?"

"6,000 square feet. That was just the public viewing area. The archives were twice that size."

"How do you know the museum disappeared?"

"Not the museum, the artifacts. The museum was in a bank, a throwback to the old days when a bank was part of the community, culturally speaking. The museum was a draw. And advertising for the bank. Now, in this age of electronics and Wi-Fi, no one goes to banks."

"So, no one is taking the family to see artifacts," Noonan cut in. "No patrons, no advertising of the bank."

Atka grimaced. "More than that. The museum was square footage that could be used by the bank or rented out. The museum brought in no rent revenue. It wasn't generating new clients for the bank, so it was just a financial drag. Banks do not think of culture, only profit."

"So, the museum was closed."

"Correct. The part-time curators were given severance, and some specialists were called in. They did an inventory of what was in the museum and decided where the items were to go."

"I take it the items were to go to many other museums. Were the items sold or just transferred?"

Atka smiled and shook his head. "Value is one of those terms which has many meanings, Heinz. A carved ivory whale in a gift shop will sell for, say, $100. But if it was carved by a well-known carver, it is worth more. Once it is in a museum it has value but no sales potential. The person who gave the whale to the museum might have taken a tax write-off of $1,000. But the whale carving is in the museum, not for sale on the street."

"But if it is only worth $100 on the street, how can someone take a $1,000 write-off?"

"Oh, it isn't the object that is worth the $1,000. It's how much was spent to get the artifact. Someone could claim they went to a remote area and purchased the whale from a local artist. Since the trip was a 'business trip,'" Atka made quote marks in the air with the index fingers of both hands, "the trip is a tax write-off. It's not the 'value' of the artifact," he said, again with the quote marks in the air, "that looks good on the books. It's the cost of getting the artifact. There's a lot of money in museums but it's hidden. You cannot look at the carved ivory whale as a stand-alone item. It took a lot of money to get that whale into the museum. Someone's cash."

"So," Noonan shook his head slowly, "there's a lot of room for money off the books."

"On the books too. Since you are not in the business, can I give you a quick lesson?"

"Go for it."

"Stop thinking of a museum as square footage where you can stand and view objects in glass cases. It's substantially more than that. First, all you see on the public floor is about 10% of the objects the museum has. In other words, there is only one carved whale on display but there are nine in the back room."

"Why so many objects in the back room? If the others are not as good as the one on display, why not sell them?"

"In most cases, the museum cannot. The other whales were given as donations. Sometimes there were strings attached. The object could not be sold, for instance, or if the museum closed, the artifact had to go back to the family that made the donation."

"So, the museum is stuck with the artifact?"

"It's more complicated than that. Many of the artifacts in storage are studied by scholars, artists, and academicians. Again, don't think of a museum as a large room with lots of glass cases. 90% of the artifacts are in storage and there is a significant amount of cultural information that can be gleaned from the artifacts in storage."

"And those objects have a dollar value?"

Atka laughed, "You're thinking like a cop. Again, it is a question of value. Yes, they have value. But only if the object comes with the provenance. If you took one of those ivory whales from storage to a store to pawn, you'd get about $50. With the provenance at Christie's, you might get $1,000 and if it had been owned and donated by someone important, like a Governor, maybe $5,000. In 1966, after Jaqueline Kennedy Onassis died and some of JFK's personal items went on auction. JFK's humidor sold for $575,000. I mean, Heinz, we are talking about a wooden box. It's not like a Picasso or Von Gogh you can display. And not that many people know JFK smoked four cigars a day. Everyone knows he smoked a few joints of marijuana before a narcotics conference to see its effect, but I doubt one American in a hundred knows he smoked cigars. But someone paid $575,000 for a humidor you could buy at a smoke shop for a few hundred dollars. That's the power of a provenance."

Noonan smiled. "Oh, I understand that. But what I was basically asking, is, yes, 'Where's the money?' If this museum disappeared, whatever made it go poof and gone, can't sell the objects from the museum. Just like any robbery, if you can't pawn what you stole, there's no sense in stealing it in the first place."

"You are correct," Atka said. "That's the rub, as Shakespeare would say. So why steal a museum?"

CHAPTER 3

Noonan did not have a good answer much less any answer for why someone would steal museum artifacts if there was no money in it for them. It made no sense. But people do not steal things of no value so, as Noonan knew, there had to be an ulterior source of money.

"OK," he said to Atka. "Let's try this from a different tack. The bones. The ones you were going to receive. Is there anything special about them? Or, for that matter, anything special about any of the artifacts you were supposed to get?"

Atka smiled. "That's another yes and no answer."

"I seem to be racking those up today."

"If you mean, can they be sold for a dollar amount? Very doubtful. Even if you knew where and when the bones were originally found, or stolen, there is very little you can do but return the bones to the village and rebury them. But, scientifically speaking, there is a lot of genetic information with those bones. For a good example, read any article in *National Geographics* on Pompeii. There is a lot of cultural information from the bones. Then there is the DNA in the bones. Technology is leaping forward so we do not know today what possible data we will be able to get from the bones tomorrow, in a week or a decade. Some bones are kept for that purpose."

"How about the artifacts that were supposed to come here?" Noonan twirled his pen to indicate the Municipal Museum.

"They're missing too. We didn't pay anything for the artifacts and as far as I know, no other museum in Alaska paid for any of the items."

"How about out of Alaska?"

"Good question. Bottom line is I doubt it. The museum that closed was Alaskan. The items were Alaskan. I don't see a museum in the Lower 48 opening an Alaska room. Museums are not money-makers. Every square foot of display area costs money. Why would a museum in Denver spend money to open an Alaska room?"

Noonan shook his head. "It's been my sad experience that when there is an unexplained crime, there's some money involved."

Atka smiled. "That's your world, not mine. What we have here is a failure of bones to arrive. Arrive here. Your in-laws said you were a master at solving the insolvable. I know you're on vacation but, hey, give the Municipal Museum a shot at getting our bones."

CHAPTER 4

Harrison Anderson did not look like an Alaska Native. He did not sound like an Alaska Native which, in reality, was a nothing statement. A lot of descendants of the English on the Outer Banks of North Carolina did not sound British or speak with the Outer Banks brogue or have a North Carolina accent. Anderson was dressed in jeans and a checkered, long-sleeve shirt and wore a museum tunic. He could not have been older than his mid-forties, was built like a weightlifter and had a full head of black hair. It took a moment for Anderson to shake Noonan's hand because Anderson had to strip off a pair of plastic gloves. "When you handle artifacts," he said shaking the gloves as he set them on his desk, "you must be careful. Have a seat." He indicated a leather chair in front of his desk.

"Yupik," Anderson said when Noonan asked if he was Native. "Mixed heritage. What do you know about Alaska Natives."

"What you tell me."

Anderson laughed. "Generally speaking – scattered across the *268,581 square miles* of the state – there are three Native ethnic groups, eleven distinct cultures, speaking twenty different languages with more than 50 dialects who live in eight geographical locations in more than 200 villages and communities. It's not as easy as saying if you are an Indian in Montana you are a Sioux."

Noonan chuckled. "Let's stick to the crime."

"Not one here, sorry. Not yet anyway. I'm the Cultural Specialist for the Aboriginal Artifact Commission. My job, for the moment, is to oversee all artifacts from the National Bank of Anchorage Museum and then send them on their way to other museums, libraries, and archives."

"I've been told some bones are missing."

"Captain!"

"Heinz. Until there's a crime, I'm Heinz."

"OK, Heinz. Then I'm Harrison. My father is a direct descendant of William Henry Harrison. I have his genes, so I also got his name. Heinz, there is no crime here. I don't see there is one. I mean, really! How can you steal things that cannot be sold?"

"But some museum artifacts are missing."

"All of them are missing."

"Sorry?"

"All of them. All of the artifacts, bones too, were packed up six weeks ago. We were in charge of the distribution. Last I was told they were missing from an Anchorage warehouse."

"Missing?"

"The Anchorage Warehouse is huge, Heinz. The artifact packages are small in comparison to what is stored there. The artifacts are still there. It'll just take some time to find them. Maybe 'missing' is the wrong term to use. How about 'waylaid?'"

Noonan shook his head as he opened his notebook. "You don't mind if I take notes?"

"Not at all," Anderson said. "Nothing to hide. When the decision was made by the National Bank of Anchorage to close the museum, the artifacts were inventoried and, on paper, chosen by other museums in Alaska. The bank didn't own the museum. It just provided the space for free. Once the decision was made the bank needed more mezzanine floor space, the museum was shuttered. Then the artifacts were packed. All of the packing was done at the National Bank of Anchorage Museum for the final destination museums That was to make it easy to distribute the artifacts. So, when the boxes are finally found, they will all go their separate way. The hard work has been done. Now we just have to wait for the boxes to be found."

"Are the provenances missing too?"

"Not missing, Heinz, waylaid. Yes, all provenances for all artifacts were divvied up, so to speak. The bones for the Municipal Museum and the provenances for the bones were packaged together. Nothing personal, but you cops are always looking to follow the money. There is none here. Or in a museum. Artifacts only have a cash value in the form of tax deductions for the people or companies which donate them. To make the big bucks with an artifact – not that there are big bucks in Alaska artifacts –you have to have a provenance. Do you know what a provenance is?"

Noonan wrote 'Where?' in his notebook and then said, "A provenance is a record of who bought what when and for how much."

"Exactly," Anderson leaned back in the desk chair. "When the artifacts were divided up, the provenances were included with the artifacts in the packages, so to speak."

"And you were in charge of the project?"

"I didn't put the artifacts in the boxes, no, if that's what you are asking. But I was the one who divvied up the artifacts for delivery on paper. And the provenances. I only handled the transfer paperwork. If that makes me in charge, yes, I was."

"So, there are actually many packages, correct?" Noonan was writing in his notebook. "Or collections of packages, each collection destined for a specific museum."

Anderson smiled and shook his head. "Close enough. Some of the artifacts were going to libraries. Then there are the bones. They are a bit more difficult to deal with. They will be owned, to use a legal term, by a museum but some will be initially sent to laboratories to see if any genetic material can be extracted."

Noonan looked over the notes in his notebook. "OK, I understand. Let me ask the question another way. The packages that are missing ..."

"Waylaid," Anderson cut in.

"OK, waylaid," Noonan adjusted his vocabulary. "The *waylaid* packages, what kind of volume are we talking about? That is, when they were shipped and then waylaid, how large was the shipment?"

"The large, bulky items, like baleen, paddles, blankets, paintings, sections of totem poles, and masks, were picked up by the museums where the items were to go. All of them were in the rail belt. Do you know what the rail belt is?"

Noonan chuckled. "All cities you can reach by road between Fairbanks and Homer."

"Good for you. A lot of outsiders are not familiar with the term. There was no reason to pack the large objects because they had already been picked up. All that was left were the small items, the ones in the display cases, if you will. The small items were individually packed according to museum of destination. But they were not stacked that way on the pallets. The stacking on the pallets was for balance. All totaled we had six pallets piled six feet high. About 100 square feet."

"Where did the artifacts get waylaid?"

"In a warehouse. Huge, Heinz. Almost as large as the Indiana Jones warehouse in the movie of the Lost Ark."

Noonan scratched some words on a notebook page. "But you did not actually see the loaded pallets. You just signed off on the delivery."

"Yes, I just signed off on the forms."

Noonan kind of fiddled with his pen. "The company, the transportation company. They confirmed they delivered the load and put it in the warehouse?"

Anderson shook his head. "More complicated than that. That's why it's been so hard to trace the crates. First, the men who loaded the truck trailer were day laborers. The truck was owned by a local shipping company but the driver, a teamster, was hired at the union hall. The crates were unloaded by staff at the warehouse and that's where they were mislaid."

Noonan was writing furiously. "But the crates did come out of the truck trailer, correct."

"Yup. On pallets. Six of them. You know what pallets are?"

"The wood frames under cargo. Two-by-fours with space for a forklift to move them."

"Correct. The crates on the pallets were lifted out of the back of the truck trailer with a forklift and stored in the warehouse. About a week later, when I started the paper process of breaking apart the large crates for individual shipments, the pallets with the crates could not be found in the warehouse."

"Could the crates have been shipped out of the Anchorage warehouse by mistake?"

"Doubtful. There are pretty good records for what goes in and what comes out. Doublechecked and all. No, the museum crates are still there. We just haven't been able to find them yet."

"Why were the artifacts not sent to the museums the first time. I mean, why send them to a warehouse and then separate them there?"

"Well, the first stop for the pallets was the shipping company. It was more of a space problem than efficiency. There were six pallets to load and there wasn't that much room at the bank. The bank was moving people and furniture into the former museum's space while we were struggling to get the artifacts out. As a pallet was loaded, it was sent to the shipping company's garage. Then the boxes and crates were off loaded from that one pallet and placed on one of the six pallets. It was done that way because some boxes and crates were large, others small. The pallets could not have large, heavy boxes on top of smaller ones. The final separation by museum would be done later. The final delivery was held there until all the pallets arrived in the shipping company garage. Then all six pallets, together, were taken to the warehouse in one load."

Anderson paused and then continued. "Why weren't the artifacts sent to the museums as the crates were filled? A lot of reasons. The bank wanted the space ASAP. Then, some of the museums needed time to make space available. Others wanted the artifacts to be part of their visual display and had to order new glass cases. Libraries and archives are, well, run by bureaucrats, and every order of any kind needs 34.4 signatures. Don't think of the artifacts as something you can pick up with your hand and put on a shelf." Anderson picked up his plastic gloves with the index finger and thumb of his right hand. "There are standards we all must follow. And they are written up. Those artifacts are not like used books on their way to a flea market."

Noonan chuckled. "OK. Seeing as I'm already on this matter, do you mind if I take a look around the warehouse?"

"Fine with me," Anderson said. "I don't see why not. But I've got to get permission first. Then there's the insurance question, so I'll have to call the company involved. It could take some time. I'd rather not call the Anchorage Police because, well, like I said, there is no crime here."

"Call around and let me know," Noonan said as he scribbled his cell phone number on a sheet of paper and handed it to Anderson. "I hate to work on vacation but when the alternative is hobnobbing with in-laws ..." He let the sentence hang.

"Not a problem. I've got two villages of 'em."

CHAPTER 5

Surprisingly, it took less than three hours for Noonan to get the go-ahead to visit the Anchorage Warehouse and Storage Facility.

But he had to go with the insurance broker, and he was to meet her at the front door of the establishment.

Bernice Whitcomb turned out to be a blessing in disguise. First, she represented a handful of insurance companies on the East Coast, so she did not have a proprietor interest in the waylaid museum property. She was, in essence, the paper pusher; she, personally, had nothing at risk. Second, she was personable and third, she was a font of local information. Over the years Noonan had found his best leads on loo-loo cases like this one were local newspapers and local history. With Whitcomb, he had both in one person.

Whitcomb was as black as the Ace of Spades. She stood a good four inches taller than Noonan and he was an inch over six feet. Her hair was in dreadlocks – Noonan's was white, but he still had his – and she had blood-red fingernails. As Noonan shook her hand, Whitcomb said flatly, "I never played basketball or soccer, I was born in Atlanta, and I have a Business Degree from the University of North Carolina."

Noonan chuckled. "Good for you. I ran track, was born in Virginia Beach and I have a degree in Criminology from Rutgers. So, we should get along famously."

Whitcomb smiled. "I was told you come from North Carolina. That's the South and my people are not treated well there."

Noonan chuckled again. "Well, I've from the Outer Banks and the only people who are treated well there are tourists at the check-out counter."

Now she laughed. "Well, we'll get along. There's a lot of prejudice. Not so much up here in Alaska."

"The further west you go, the fewer people care who you are."

Now she smiled broadly. "Got that right. My husband and I love this place. No one cares who you are as long as you do your job well."

Noonan shook his head comically and stuck out his hand, "Now that we've broken the ice, I'm Heinz Noonan. And it's Heinz until there's a crime."

She shook his hand. "Bernice. Or Bernie. Either works for me. All I've been told is that you are looking for the museum shipment. So am I. It's been a few weeks and the office in Baltimore is getting nervous."

Noonan indicated a stack of crates in the front of the warehouse, and they settled against the wood wall. Then he opened his notebook. "Why don't you bring me up to speed with what you know."

"First," she began as she handed Noonan a manila folder, "it's important you understand Alaska is not Kansas. We don't do things the Lower 48 way up here. If it works, we do it."

Noonan chuckled again. "I've been married to an Alaskan for 40 years. And I've got 40 years' worth of vacation time up here, big city, village, bush, and Arctic. It will be hard to surprise me with the Alaskan way do doing things."

Whitcomb tapped the envelope with a red fingernail. "The disappearance is odd and there is a lot of oddness in the delivery and storage. Overall, I guess I have to tell you two little stories before I get to the disappearance."

"I'm listening."

"Like I said, Alaska is not Kansas. In the Lower 48, where you come from, there are all kinds of storage houses. There are facilities for frozen foods, refrigerated foods, fruits and vegetables about to be shipped as cargo, trucking packaging, containers, secure facilities for armored cars, and whatever. Depending on what you are shipping, you go to a facility that specializes in that item. You get your frozen food from one facility and that facility only. Same with cartons of clothes or liquor or canned goods. Depending on where a truck is going, it might go to three or four different warehouses. Then there are the containers. Do you know what a container is?"

Noonan pointed to a pile of containers in the distance. "Those are containers, some are coming loaded and others are going out empty."

"Yup. All of the containers coming into Anchorage contain products for Alaska. In the Lower 48, a container might come off a railcar and have product destined for a whole bunch of cities near the railyard. Not so up here. Everything coming in here is for Alaska. Anchorage products get distributed here. Fairbanks items go by truck north. For smaller communities and villages, it goes to the Anchorage Airport."

"I understand," Noonan said as he tried to get his pen to work. It wouldn't so Whitcomb handed him one. "I was told you are always looking for pens. So, I brought a pocketful."

Noonan took the pen. "Not looking for one now." He tapped his notebook. "Now, the point of this story ..." He let the sentence hang.

Whitcomb swept her finger from the pile of containers to the door of the warehouse. "In the Lower 48, the containers would immediately go from the railyard, let's say to a warehouse destination in a city. Like a shipment of shoes. The container with the shoes would go to the warehouse that handled clothing where it would be opened, and the shoes divided out for the shoe stores in the area. Same for canned goods. Umbrellas, flowers, chips, equipment. Whatever. But not up here. In Anchorage, everything comes here, to this warehouse, and is sorted out here by destination. That's why the museum shipment came here. It was going to be divided out, museum by museum, and packaged for shipment with the cargo for that city."

Noonan tapped his notebook. "So, the shoes and canned goods and potato chips for say, Kenai, would all go in one truck."

"Kenai is a bad example because it gets lots of trucks. Say for Cordova, one container would have a variety of goods. The perishables would go by cargo plane. Everything else would go by barge. Cordova is landlocked."

"What you are saying is there is a lot of activity in the warehouse so having the museum shipment go missing is understandable."

"Understandable is not the word I would use, but, yes, you get the picture."

"OK, you said you had two stories. What's the second story?"

Whitcomb waggled a finger in Noonan's direction. "Have to move slowly here. Let me finish up the first story."

"I'm all ears."

"Funny. I voted for Perot." She tapped Noonan's notebook with her right forefinger nail. "The cargo is actually only part of the first story. There are three other aspects to keep in mind. First, is the paperwork. All cargo coming into the warehouse is logged in. All cargo going out is logged out. All cargo in the warehouse is identified by location. So, during a normal delivery, there is incoming paperwork, storage paperwork and outgoing paperwork."

"Understandable."

"Sure, when it works. But there is a human factor here. The cargo coming into Anchorage arrives in trucks and railcars, in containers, by United States mail, FedEx, UPS, and individuals. It is not a smooth process and all the people who are bringing the cargo in have their own paperwork. So, when you talk about paperwork, it is a *tsunami.* For the museum cargo, for instance, there was the National Bank of Anchorage paperwork, the paperwork from the teamster who drove the truck here, the paperwork from the crew who loaded the museum cargo, and the paperwork from the warehouse crew who unloaded the cargo. Then there is the paperwork for where the cargo is being stored in the warehouse. And the insurance paperwork and, not in the case of the museum, if there is any hazardous material it has to be checked for safety."

Noonan kept writing as he spoke. "So, there is a lot of paperwork, and it is possible for things to go missing."

"Correct. And six pallets are minuscule compared to what goes in and out of this warehouse."

"So, it is possible for something to get lost?"

"Happens all the time. What is different here is that the museum cargo has not been found. That's odd."

"Any chance it was stolen?"

Whitcomb smiled. "And now to my second story. I'll have to segue."

"Proceed."

"If you want to sell your home, that structure has four values. One is what you are asking. Another is what the city says the property is worth for city taxes. The third is what the appraiser says other similar homes are valued at, and the fourth is what you actually sell it for."

"Understood."

Whitcomb took a deep breath. "Selling a home is easy because the final price will be determined when everyone involved finds the price reasonable. The home will be mortgaged for that amount and insured for that amount and taxed for that amount. Museum artifacts are very different. Rarely does a museum buy an artifact. Museums *acquire* artifacts. John and Mary Smith donate an artifact and the museum accepts it. The museum does not state the value of the artifact, only that the Smith family donated it. In the provenance," she stalled for a moment, "you do know what a provenance is?"

"Yes. It's a record of the history of the artifact."

"Right. It might record how much was paid for the artifact in the first place. Usually not. What is important is that the Smiths *owned* the artifact they were donating to the museum. What they tell the IRS is their own business. Everything the Smiths donated to the museum is recorded in museum paperwork, but the only dollar figures are if the Smiths donated money to the museum. Or if they left money in a will for the museum. But the key item here is the paperwork does not record the *value* of any artifact. So, if you ask me how much the insurance company will have to pay for the missing artifacts, it gets very dicey very quickly."

"Why is that?"

"Because, like I said before with the four values of a house being sold, it's complicated. What I have, what the insurance covers, is the entire museum shipment. It was insured for ten million dollars. That's the *estimated* replacement cost. If every object in the museum had to be replaced, or purchased, it is estimated to cost ten million dollars."

"Who made that estimate?"

"The Aboriginal Artifact Commission. Our company would never pay that. It's kind of a pie-in-the-sky number. But with ten million on paper, as you can understand, my company is concerned."

"I can see that," Noonan replied.

"Now, I must continue with my second story."

Noonan waved her to continue.

"What makes everything complicated is that the provenances for the individual artifacts are with the artifacts."

Noonan nodded. "You mean, paper proof that John and Mary Smith gave an artifact."

"Yes, with no dollar value attributed to the artifact. The replacement estimate still exists and it's in the possession of the Aboriginal Artifact Commission. If the museum artifacts are not found, the insurance payment will be based on that paperwork."

"Would payment go to the Aboriginal Artifact Commission or the museums?"

Whitcomb smiled. "Thinking like a cop, I see. If payment must be made, it will probably be in checks to the museums. The Aboriginal Artifact Commission never owned the artifacts. It just did the paperwork to distribute the artifacts. If it gets anything, it would be a fee that was negotiated by individual museums. But don't go assuming there are ten million dollars on the table to be divided up. If that money is ever paid it is going to be a long time coming. A very long time."

CHAPTER 6

If Noonan had been asked – beforehand – to describe the physical characteristic of men who would be employed to work in a warehouse, he would never have had Alberto Mutofa and Giuseppe Abramowitz in mind. Mutofa was Samoan, and so clearly Samoan you could tell in a glance at 50 yards. Abramowitz could have slithered down a rabbit hole with room to spare. Surprisingly, Mutofa was a forklift operator and Abramowitz a floor supervisor.

"Got all the time in the world for you," Mutofa said without an accent of any kind.

"Same here," retorted Abramowitz with a New Orleans drawl that stretched into the next month. "Time and a half after five so ask your questions r-e-a-l-l-y s-l-o-w."

Noonan chuckled while Whitcomb handed them the museum paperwork. "You remember this shipment?"

Mutofa shook his head. "Can't forget it, what was your name again?"

"Heinz. Keeping it casual."

"Better than when I get called. Yeah, I remember it. So does Abe," he pointed at Abramowitz. "We've been through this before."

"Still missing, too." Abramowitz said as he pointed that the paperwork. "Heinz, it is Heinz, yeah?"

"Yeah."

"Heinz, I'll, we'll, say the same thing we said to her," he indicated Whitcomb, "and the three or four others who asked the same question. The truck came in, we were handed this paperwork, and we unloaded the truck. Not a large load. Six pallets. Moved them into a space and that was that. When it came time to move the load, what, three weeks later, the space where the pallets were supposed to be had a different load there."

Noonan fiddled with a pen on a notebook page. "OK, let's take this slowly. How well do you remember this particular load?" He pointed at the Aboriginal Artifact Commission shipping invoice.

"Not at all," Mutofa said as he shook his head. "We move hundreds of pallets a week. Some from trucks, some onto trucks, some into containers, some out of containers. All I can tell you," he said pointing at the paperwork, "is six pallets came out of that truck."

"Is there any chance there was any other cargo in the truck?"

"No way to know," added Abramowitz. "We don't empty trucks or containers or box cars. We transfer the pallets we sign for. If the paperwork says to unload six pallets, that's what we unload. This delivery," he tapped the paperwork, "was weeks ago, Heinz. Weeks. The only thing I can tell you is the truck from," he looked at the paperwork, "Chugach Shipping, Ltd. arrived, and we removed six pallets. Then we signed we had received the pallets. The driver signed. The doors to the back of the truck were closed. He drove off. We moved the pallets into the warehouse."

"Was there a place assigned in advance for the six pallets?"

"Not the way you mean it," Mutofa cut in. "This place," he allowed his hand to sweep to indicate the interior of the warehouse, "has all kinds of cargo. Some of it is going to be transferred within hours of when it came in. Other cargo is stored until there is enough to put in a specific container for a specific destination. Some is stored for weeks until some bill is paid, or some paperwork comes in. Do we lose cargo? Sure. Every once in a while. But we usually find it."

"Eventually," added Abramowitz. "But stolen, not so much. All cargo comes in with paperwork. All cargo goes out with paperwork. No one walks into the warehouse and leaves with any pallets without exit paperwork. That's what we call it. The outgoing cargo." He tapped the paperwork. "This cargo is still here. We just haven't found it yet."

Noonan thought for a moment and then asked, "Once the pallets came in, they were set in a certain place, correct?"

Both men nodded.

"Then the pallets had to have been moved. Is there paperwork that indicates where the pallets were moved to?"

Abramowitz nodded. "Yes, there is paperwork, a map so to speak, of where things are. Nothing gets moved around the warehouse without that paperwork. These pallets," again he tapped the paperwork, "I can't say. It's odd we could lose six pallets."

"Any chance the pallets just had empty crates?"

"Doubtful," Mutofa said. "I mean, the weight of the crates is listed on the paperwork. I can't say for sure that the weight was correct, but I would know if the load was empty. I would be able to feel it as I drove the forklift. Whatever was offloaded, the poundage, was there."

Noonan thought for a moment. "OK, so the pallets were heavy when they were offloaded. Did you," he indicated Mutofa, "take them directly to where they were to be stored?"

"Can't say. Again, everything in the warehouse moves around. There is a paper trail, I guess you could call it, of all the shipments when they came in and where they were stored or moved. It's not as though the pallets came in, we put them against the wall in 38B and they stayed there until they disappeared." He looked at the paperwork. "This is just the incoming paperwork. The cargo coming in."

"Can I get a copy of the movement of the pallets once they were in the warehouse?"

"Don't see why not," Abramowitz pointed to the paperwork. "But it will not be listed as pallets from the museum. It will be listed by the owner of the pallets, the," he read the words, "Aboriginal Artifact Commission. But I have to tell you that you will need some kind of paperwork from this Aboriginal Artifact Commission to see any records. I know the front office and they are suspicious of everyone."

"Particularly," Mutofa added, "when it comes to missing shipments."

"I can understand that," Noonan said as he smiled. "One more thing. How many people work on the floor in the warehouse?"

"Depends on the day, the season, the orders. Some days we have 60, some full-time, some part-time. Middle of winter, maybe 20."

"But there is a record of everyone who worked here during the time the pallets were here."

"Should be," chuckled Mutofa. "If they wanted to be paid."

CHAPTER 7

Harrison Anderson was not surprised to see Noonan and Bernice Whitcomb back in his office.

"I got the call," he said as he handed them a sheet of paper. "You'll need this to get the information you want from the Anchorage Warehouse and Storage Facility. Best of luck."

Noonan took the sheet of paper and looked it over. Then he said, "Just a few questions while we're here."

Anderson spread his arms wide, "Not a problem."

Noonan flipped through his notebook, "Chugach Shipping, Ltd., the shipping company that picked up the museum artifacts, who hired the company?"

"We did. We put out a bid and they got it."

Noonan continued. "And as far as you know, the artifacts from the bank went to the warehouse of the," Noonan had to look at the name of the shipping company again, "Chugach Shipping as the boxes of artifacts were being separated out. Then, the boxes and crates went to the Chugach Shipping warehouse where they were loaded on six pallets that went to the warehouse in one shipment."

Anderson responded as he nodded his head. "Yes, the six pallets went directly to the warehouse from the Chugach Shipping garage."

"Where they disappeared?"

"Waylaid, not disappeared," Anderson smiled. "It is not reasonable for artifacts to be stolen. There's no money in artifacts." He pointed to Whitcomb. "I hope she told you that. If there were money in artifacts, yes, I'd say they could have been stolen. But in answer to your question, I assume the load, the six pallets from the garage of Chugach Shipping went directly to the warehouse. I looked over the paperwork at the warehouse. Six pallets came in. Six pallets left the warehouse of Chugach Shipping. I'm assuming they were the same pallets."

"Do you have any problem with me talking with the Chugach Shipping people?" Noonan asked.

"Not at all." Anderson opened a folder on his desk. He took out a sheet of paper and ran it through his printer. "Here you go. Regina Hemmingway is the contact there. She's the owner of the operation. Classy lady."

CHAPTER 8

Regina Hemmingway was a classy lady.

A *very* classy lady.

Her office throbbed culture. Yupik, Inuit and Aleut cultures. She was an elegant six-foot-two with jet-black hair that hung to her waist. Her makeup was impeccable, and she had long, white fingernails. Her desk was a spread of files under three small slabs of jade. She also had an ivory letter opener and an Aleut basket for in/out paperwork. The pictures on her wall were a mix of cultural icons, photos of Native dancers and some moiety masks. In the upper corner of her office was an Inuit skin drum. Her office wall was plastered with certificates of merits along with quite a few grip-and-grin photographs.

"You are as good as a museum," Noonan said as he pointed around the room at the artifacts.

"Part of my heritage, Inupiat and Athabaskan. In the old days," she gave Noonan a humorous look to hint at his age, "we were just *Indians*." She slurred the word *Indians*. "Today we are a respected people." She smiled. "Which is why I was pleased to get the bid for moving the artifacts. We bid very low, took a loss, for the honor."

"I'm sure your ancestors would have appreciated that," Noonan said.

"Oh, they do. No one is ever gone, Captain. It is 'Captain,' isn't it?"

Noonan smiled as he took out his notebook. "Only when there is a crime. Right now, there is no crime so I'm just 'Heinz.'"

"Then I'm Regina. And you," she pointed at Bernice Whitcomb, "are the insurance lady."

"Same one," Whitcomb said. "We're," she used her index finger to flick from Noonan to herself, "following the path of the artifacts."

"A good way to investigate. Harrison said you would be by."

"You are a close friend?" Noonan asked. "With Harrison, I mean."

"We here at Chugach are quite supportive of the Aboriginal Artifact Commission. For some shippers, artifacts are just 'things in crates.'" She let her right handshake back and forth like a fish swimming through the water. "My brother and I – we're a family operation – take pride in our heritage. To us, anything coming to or from the Aboriginal Artifact Commission is special and should be treated with respect."

"So," Noonan said as his pen hovered over a page in his notebook. "You've done work for the Commission before?"

"A lot. But then again, it's been small loads. We are a six-truck operation. Not one of the big operators. Small customers occasionally need small loads delivered: a desk, some shelving, or loads of books. A lot of it comes from out of town. There might be, say, a dozen boxes of books from the University Press in Fairbanks. When we are in Fairbanks for a delivery or pickup, we include the books. At the same time, we might take some artifacts from the Aboriginal Artifact Commission to Fairbanks. We'd store the artifacts here until we have a shipment north."

"Shipping of artifacts?" Noonan looked surprised. "I was under the impression that once an artifact was in a museum, that's where it stayed."

Hemmingway chuckled. "Heinz, right?"

Noonan nodded.

"Heinz, the best museums do not have the same old same old. If they did, patrons would arrive, see all there was to see, and not come back. A museum is a living beast, always changing always growing. Objects get moved around inside the museum and traded from other museums Like specials. King Tut is a good example. All of King Tut's artifacts are not in one museum, they travel. Sometimes all together to a large museum, sometimes parceled out to smaller ones. There are special shows all the time. Again and again, Heinz, a museum is a living, breathing entity. We here at Chugach Shipping are proud to be on the front line of that living and breathing. And in Alaska, the objects being moved around are not numerous. Or heavy. We do quite a bit of business with the Aboriginal Artifact Commission because we don't charge much, and we stockpile the artifacts until we schedule loads out of Anchorage. Or we bring artifacts back."

Noonan muttered a *humm,* or *ahhh,* and went on to his next question. "Never lost a load before?"

"We haven't lost this load yet. The artifacts came here and then they were moved to the warehouse."

"And all of the artifacts came here, in crates and boxes, a delivery at a time, correct?"

"Correct. Yes, they came here, but not all at once. But we shipped them to the warehouse all at once."

"Did Harrison Anderson do oversight of the archive loading on the pallets?"

"No. He oversaw the operation. He might have been in the National Bank of Anchorage a time or two but not long. But he was here when the pallets were loaded to go to the warehouse. My brother, Johnathan, was in charge of the overall operation on a daily basis. At the bank and here. It was an agonizing process. Do you have the time for some nuts and bolts?"

Noonan raised his hands in the Italian expression of 'Go on.'

"Moving the artifacts was not a one-shot deal. It was quite convoluted. Let's just forget about the process of asking which museums wanted what. Once all the artifacts had been given a destination, so to speak, they had to be packaged for shipment. The first function was to pair the provenance with the artifact. You do know what a provenance is?"

"Yes."

"Then the largest objects, the ones that could not reasonable be put in boxes, were picked up by the separate museums These were objects like wooden artwork, paddles, baleen, paintings, blankets, pieces of totem poles, masks, firearms, and clocks. These were easy objects to distribute because the staff from the museums where the objects were going showed up and took them away. We also parceled out the display cases in the sense we knew which museums wanted them and as they were emptied, staff from the other museums came and removed them. None went to the bush so none of the display cases had to be sent as air cargo. I think we dumped about one-third of them because it would have been more expensive to repair them than replace them."

She continued. "Once the large artifacts left and their provenance were paired, the small artifacts and their provenances were wrapped according to their destination, each delivery in a separate cocoon of bubble wrap. Then each cocoon was put in an appropriately sized crate. Smaller crates were put in larger boxes. Then the boxes were put on a pallet, one because that was all the room we had in the National Bank of Anchorage. This was important because some of the artifacts were incredibly delicate, so it took a professional to do the hands-on. My brother, Jonathan handled the nuts and bolts of the operation in the museum. He's been doing jobs like that for years, so he knows what he is doing. There was not a lot of room, that is, floor space, in the old museum so, as crates were filled, they were put on that one pallet. Then they were sent here. We unloaded that pallet and sent it back to the museum. Then we parceled out the boxes on six pallets here by size and weight."

"Why weren't the filled crates sent out immediately?"

"Our contract was only for the extraction, so to speak, from the museum. We were to close the museum and send the artifacts all together to the Anchorage Warehouse and Storage Facility. Then the pallets would be picked up by another contractor who would separate out the individual deliveries for the individual museums. It was the Aboriginal Artifact Commission's way of spreading around the money. All of us involved in the distribution were small contractors."

"Was the separating and repacking to be done in the warehouse?"

"Presumably not. We did not have that contract so I can't say for sure. Most likely the pallets of artifacts would be taken to another location and divided up. Our contract was only to close the museum, package the artifacts as needed, load the pallets, and deliver them to the Anchorage Warehouse."

Noonan looked at his notebook. "Except for the large objects and the display cases. Those were picked up by someone and transported to a museum."

Regina chuckled. "For the largest objects, yes. But don't think museum artifacts are like books on a shelf, and you can point to six books and say, 'Those go to Bethel.' It's not that simple. Not only that, but there were also artifacts in closets, file cabinets, desk drawers and other repositories no one knew about until the inventory was started."

"Isn't that odd for a museum?"

"Not really. Rather, for the Los Angeles Museum of Natural History, yes. But not for a small museum with a part-time staff. And don't forget, there were artifacts still coming in and artifacts yet to be processed and artifacts that had been sent out for repair. It was a painstaking process made worse by the time constraints. It took months. As the boxes were filled and removed from the museum, we stored them here."

Noonan shook his head. "The way I hear it, you stored the artifacts here and then shipped the six loaded pallets to the warehouse. After that, you had nothing to do with the load."

"Correct. Crate by box by whatever, they were assembled in the old museum. Then they came here, piecemeal, on one pallet." She sighed. "But just saying that makes it sound simple. It wasn't. There was still some sorting done here. The crates, boxes, and packages from the museum were not packed by size but by content. For instance, all of the ivory carvings were divided out and packed separately for different museums. Under normal packing circumstances, so to speak, you'd divide the load by city. That way all the Bethel-bound artifacts would be separate from the Fairbanks-bound artifacts. That was the way the next phase, the transport, was going to be. But not our part. We had to balance the load on the pallets by weight so there would be no tip-overs. Once the load was balanced, it was shipped to the Anchorage Warehouse and Storage Facility. Basically, the artifacts came in by size and content as the work proceeded in the bank and we divided them out and loaded them on six pallets here by size and weight. We had to have all of the large crates on one pallet and the smaller ones on another. We didn't want heavy crates crushing smaller boxes."

"So, you were basically collecting artifact boxes and crates so they could go to the Anchorage Warehouse and Storage Facility in one delivery."

"Correct. We stacked the crates on the pallets by size and weight, wrapped them all with plastic sheets and sent them to the Anchorage Warehouse." She handed Noonan some paperwork. "I know you want to see this. These are the transport documents."

Noonan was looking over the sheets of paper when Bernice Whitcomb added a few tidbits. "Heinz, I talked with the men who loaded the pallets. The pallets were labeled for the warehouse and loaded into the truck. The pallet piles, so to speak, had been growing in size for a few weeks so everyone knew where the museum artifacts were in the garage here. This place is small so there are no cubbyholes where six pallets can be hidden, just in case you think there might have been a switch. They loaded the pallets into the truck. The truck went directly to the Anchorage Warehouse. The load paperwork matches, and the time matches. The truck could not have stopped along the way."

Noonan looked at Hemmingway. "The driver of the truck, was he an employee?"

"My brother, Johnathan, yes. The men who loaded the pallets into our truck here were part-time or seasonal. When we need them, we hire them. The economy's been good, so they've been spending a lot of time here."

"When they do not work here, where do they work?"

"Everywhere. Some of them drive trucks and some load cargo on trucks or the Alaska Railroad. At any one time we have a dozen or so here in the back."

"Do you actually know which men loaded the museum artifacts?"

"No. They are paid by the hour and do the work needed. The best I could do is get you a list of names who were working that day. But there is no way to break it down further. Even if I could, the list would not help you. I mean, we are talking about loading six pallets. Small as we are, that's still a small load. On top of that, it's been weeks. I doubt anyone will ever remember the loading."

CHAPTER 9

"Frankly, Heinz," Bernice Whitcomb said as she stirred her coffee. "I really do not know why you are so interested in this case." The two were sitting in the coffee shop of the Loussac Library. "I mean, there is nothing for you here. There is no crime. All that's missing are artifacts and they have no street value. 'Street value' I guess is the term you use."

Noonan was working on his last coffee of the day. It was pushing 11 in the morning, and he had learned over the years to avoid coffee after the noon hour – unless it was a *Naugahyde Night* when he was waiting for forensic results from a laboratory on the West Coast. Or worse, overseas. When he had to stay awake, coffee was the key. Or worse, horror stories by MaryAnn Poll or Cil Gregoire. Then he was *really* awake.

"Bernice, I smell money. There is a lot more happening here than just missing artifacts. The missing artifacts are just to lure someone away from the real crime. What that real crime is, I do not know. Rather, I do not know yet. There is something else going on here."

Whitcomb smiled. "Cops! I've been dealing with cops for years. Every time there is an insurance claim, I've got to fill out the paperwork and send it to the police. Then I have to follow a policeman – or policewoman – around the alleged crime scene looking for clues that the water damage or fire damage is not an insurance scam. Sometimes it is, but most of the time not."

Noonan stirred the last of his coffee. "Bernice! I've been coming to Alaska for 40 years. I have relatives here. Anchorage is a small town. I mean, compared to cities in the Lower 48. Anchorage has about, what, 300,000 people with 100,000 of those on the military base or in the bedroom communities on the far side of the base."

Whitcomb chuckled, "Or down the highway to the south, Girdwood. You are right. We're also different than cities in the Lower 48 in two other ways. For the record, of course, because we are talking the possibility of crime. You can see 90% of the city of Anchorage from the top of a skyscraper which, in Anchorage, is all of about 20 stories. And, yup, we only have 200,000 folks in the 120-odd blocks from Ship Creek to Rabbit Creek to the south, but we will see one million tourists between June first and September 15th."

Noonan chuckled. "Don't I know that. Whenever I come up in the summer, I can't get a restaurant table downtown. But the flipside is important. There is no better place to spend the summer than Alaska. Eighty degrees is a very warm day. It can get up to 125 in Arizona or New Mexico during the summer. I can also fish for salmon and halibut here. A lot of people in North Carolina don't even know what a halibut is."

Whitcomb chuckled. "Well, that's not the only place. I've got relatives in Green Valley and friends in Flagstaff, so I know. But you are right, Anchorage is a small town. At the same time, we do have crime here and there are very sophisticated thieves walking among us. The one thing Alaska has going for law enforcement is whatever you steal is hard to get out of state. You can't just put the ill-gotten goods in a truck and drive across a state line. If you wanted to get those artifacts out of Anchorage, they would have to go by plane, ship, or truck. Don't forget, we are talking six pallets. That's a load."

"Oh, I understand that. Did you check with the airport to see if any load that size had been flown out?"

"Routine, Heinz. Routine. Checking with the planes was child's play, so to speak. The bulk of the cargo on planes, other than tourists and their luggage, is coming into Anchorage. The big shipments, cargo-wise, are going into the bush. Why artifacts would be sent into the bush I do not know but I did check outgoing cargo manifests. All loads checked out. I paid particular attention to any shipments out of the Anchorage Warehouse. Nothing unusual and just a few loads on pallets. I also checked with the barge lines, TOTE for instance. Nothing unusual and most of that cargo had been ordered last year. You do know that most villages north of the Aleutians are only serviced by barges for about 80 days during the summer, between the time the rivers break and before they freeze up."

"And no train track linkage with Canada."

"Right. There is no train line out of Alaska, I know you know that but I'm just being thorough."

"Good. How about the trucking?"

"That was a bit more difficult to check. But again, the bulk of the shipments are coming into Alaska, not leaving. Border folks are pretty good at spotting suspicious items on both sides, American and Canadian. All paperwork matched and I looked over the spread sheets. The only glitch, so to speak, was outgoing personal cargo. An oil worker who lived in Anchorage might have been transferred to Houston, so he and his family packed up and left. If they left with a U-Haul, they could have slipped six pallets into the trailer and put furniture in front of the pallets. Could have happened but, Heinz, there's no money in artifacts. Why would anyone ship the artifacts out of town?"

"That," Noonan said as he opened his notebook, "is a very good question. Let's concentrate on the obvious. We only know three things for sure. One, with the closure of the museum, the artifacts were parceled out to a number of museums and archives, and the paper transfer was handled by the Aboriginal Artifact Commission. Two, the artifacts were packed with their individual provenances into crates or boxes or whatever for those museums and archives. Three, one at a time or in small numbers, over time, the crates or boxes were transferred to the Chugach Shipping Ltd. garage where the load was balanced out for transfer to the Anchorage Warehouse. No one disputes those facts."

Noonan took his last sip of coffee and continued. "That leaves three possibilities. One, someone substituted the artifact pallets in the Chugach Shipping garage for another shipment to the Anchorage warehouse. It would simply be a paperwork switch. The people loading the Chugach truck didn't know what was on the pallets. It was just another shipment. The pallets could have been loaded in the light of day, so to speak, and taken to some other location and stored. The driver may not have even been aware he was stealing artifacts. He was just driving six pallets somewhere. He was paid and that was it."

Whitcomb fiddled with a pen over her yellow dog notepad. "A possibility. Yes, I agree about the shipping out of the Chugach garage. But there are problems with that scenario. Everything in and out of that facility has paperwork. Yes, paperwork can be adjusted but you have to be really good at it. On top of that, just supposing the pallets were slipped out of the Chugach garage, the bad boys and girls would have to know we would be checking every trip between the time the pallets were shipped to the garage and when they went to the Anchorage warehouse. I talked with the six drivers who worked for Chugach and looked over their paperwork. A lot of trips but nothing suspicious. They are a small operation, so a lot of their shipments were modest in size. Yes, the pallets could have been shipped out. I checked with the delivery locations and got confirmation of arrival and the paperwork matched. Some were construction sites; others were refrigerated items like fish and crab. There were also some crates of books, clothing, and shoes. Not for big stores like Walmart or Costco. Those stores have their own trucks. Smaller operations. All the paperwork matches and none of the drivers said they went to an odd place and dropped on pallets with no paperwork."

"OK," Noonan fiddled with his pen. "Another possibility is the artifact pallets made it to the Anchorage Warehouse. We talked to the men who unloaded the pallets. They said the pallets were heavy, not empty. Now, there could have been some kind of paperwork substitution at the Anchorage Warehouse. A delivery came in and it was unloaded and placed in a specific location where the artifacts were supposed to be. We'll have to go back to the warehouse and follow the paperwork trail but, for the moment, we have to assume the artifact pallets made it into the warehouse."

Whitcomb chewed on her pen. "That warehouse is massive. It is quite possible the paperwork for the location was not accurate and the artifacts were mistakenly shipped out. I know that's happened before. It would not be hard to slip something out of town. See, the bulk of the cargo containers headed to Seward are empty. Did you know that?"

This took Noonan by surprise. "No, I did not know that."

Whitcomb smiled. "Again, the bulk of the cargo is coming into Anchorage. The paperwork for that cargo, in and out of Anchorage, is pretty specific when it comes to planes and trucks. Not so much with ships. Particularly cargo ships. Thousands of full cargo containers come north on barges. Some land in Seward and come to Anchorage by rail, other barges go directly to the Port of Anchorage. Depends. But once those containers are unloaded and emptied in the Anchorage Warehouse, the containers are stacked for shipment back to whatever company owns them. No one checks to see if the empty containers are really empty. If you were a very clever operator, you could slip those six pallets into an empty container and secure the load to the inside walls. Then someone could empty the container before it made it back to the company that owned the container. Maybe in Seward."

Noonan shook his head. "A possibility but doubtful. Again, the artifacts have no value. I can see something like that happening if what was being smuggled out had a dollar value."

Whitcomb nodded. "I agree. What's the third possibility?"

"The initial switch was made at the bank. Maybe, box by crate, the artifacts were not loaded at all. Some weights were put in the crates to give them an indication of heaviness. Someone at Chugach Shipping or the Anchorage Warehouse discovered the weights and dumped the entire load. Better to say the load was mislaid or lost rather than your company got bamboozled. I mean, there would be no loss to either Chugach Shipping or the Anchorage Warehouse."

Whitcomb shook her head. "I'm not going to buy that possibility. Regina Hemmingway is a no-nonsense Native. I don't see her being snookered with a substitution. I'll bet she had her fingerprints on the artifacts every inch of the way from the abandoned museum to her garage. Nice try, Heinz, but I don't see your third possibility working."

"Maybe not. But what we have are six pallets of missing artifacts. They are somewhere and why they were stolen makes no sense. I suggest we do what good cops do."

"What's that?"

"Go back to the beginning and start looking again."

CHAPTER 10

Choi Walton, the National Bank of Anchorage liaison who had worked with the Aboriginal Artifact Commission, had no problem meeting with Noonan and Whitcomb. She was friendly, knowledgeable, and outgoing. She was also a bit apologetic. "If it had been my call," she told Noonan and Whitcomb, "I'd have left the museum where it was. But that's not the way things worked out. Sorry."

Whitcomb nodded. "Things do happen. As you probably know, the artifacts have disappeared. 'Stolen' is not a word I want to use so, for the moment, 'disappeared,' is how I refer to the artifacts."

"Small town," Walton said as she looked at Noonan. "I hear you are from out of town."

"North Carolina," Noonan said. "On the coast. As far as you can get from Alaska and still speak English."

Walton laughed. "Nice touch. I'm a bit different. Born in Alaska and grew up with my father and mother in Hong Kong. They're still there. I'm here. Anchorage National Bank needed someone who could handle international accounts and I jumped at the opportunity. Now I'm back where I belong."

Noonan smiled. "We are all comfortable somewhere. Now, regarding the museum, let me tell you what I've been told, and you stop me when I go wrong."

"Telling a cop when he goes wrong?! That'll be a first for me!"

Noonan pulled out his notebook. "What I've been told is the bank needed the museum footage for office space, so the museum had to close."

"Correct. The museum was not owned by the bank but provided the space for free. The museum has been here for about 20 years. Two years ago, the man who started the museum died. He had been bankrolling the operation for years. When he died, the money stopped. His heirs didn't want to fund the museum, so a local nonprofit took over to see if it could raise money to keep the museum afloat. It couldn't. Then the bank needed the room and that killed the operation."

"What was the name of the man who had bankrolled the museum?" Noonan asked.

"William Chambers. An old Boston family. Widower. No children. He left his money to his siblings."

"I see," Noonan said as he fiddled with his pen. "The nonprofit that was set up, who was on it?"

"It wasn't an operational organization. By that I mean, it did not have a staff who managed day-to-day affairs. They were just looking for funds. The day-to-day operation was done by volunteers and overseen by some part-time staff paid by the Aboriginal Artifact Commission. Harrison Anderson, I know you've met him, was the prime mover. He's the one who made sure things held together as long as they did. There were three other Board members. One of them you've already met, Regina Hemmingway. The other was her brother, Johnathan Hemmingway, and the fourth was a pencil claimant." She looked at Noonan expectantly. "Do you know what a pencil claimant is?"

Noonan smiled. "I know my Alaska Gold Rush history. A pencil claimant is someone who signs a paper saying someone else represents them."

"Correct," Walton said. "You need four names for a nonprofit in Alaska. The two Hemmingways and Harrison were naturals. The fourth was someone in the Senior Home for Pioneers here in Anchorage. I think he's Regina and Johnathan's uncle. Nice man. Met him once. Clearly has Alzheimer's."

"So," Noonan said as he scribbled in his notebook, "both short-time and long-term management was handled, basically, by three people?"

Walton smiled as she shook her head. "I've got to be careful with cops, Captain."

"Heinz."

"What?"

"Heinz. Until there's a crime, I'm just Heinz."

"OK, then I'm Choi. I have three answers. First answer, yes. Both short- and long-term management was with the three. Second answer, there was no long-term management issue. The museum was going to close. The only management issues were who was going to get the artifacts and how the artifacts were going to get to those museums and archives. Third answer usually involves money. Heinz, there is no money in a museum. What are called 'assets' have been donated. The museum did not pay for them."

Noonan looked up from his notebook. "How about money as in a checking account?"

"Not much. I closed out the account. When William Chambers died, the bank took his name off the museum account and put on Harrison Anderson. There might have been all of $5,000. When the decision was made to close the museum, what money that was left, still about $5,000, was put in a check for the Aboriginal Artifact Commission."

Noonan made a note and then asked, "Were you here when the artifacts were paired with the provenances?"

Walton smiled. "I'm pleased a cop knows what a provenance is. Yes, I was here. No, anticipating your next question, I was not looking over anyone's shoulder. It took about two months to remove the artifacts from the exhibit cases and storage and pair them with the provenances. At the same time, someone, who I assume was Harrison Anderson or someone from his staff, was putting together the wish list from the museums and archives. The first shipment out of the museum was the management paperwork. No artifacts and no provenances. Where it went, I do not know. I assume it went to the Chugach Shipping garage."

"What do you mean by 'management paperwork?'" Whitcomb asked. "This is the first time I've heard of it."

"That's because it's not missing," Walton said casually. "As far as I know the file cabinets are in Aboriginal Artifact Commission offices." She quickly looked at Noonan. "But there are no provenances there. It's just the day-to-day operation paperwork. Budget spreadsheets, letters to and from researchers, invites and RSVPs from fundraising, electricity and solid waste service receipts. That kind of paperwork just goes into storage. Seven years later, you can dump it."

A dull gong sounded in the deepest recesses of Noonan's cerebellum. "This paperwork," he asked. "Were there references to bank accounts?"

"Don't know. I doubt it. Rent was free and help was free. No one was charged to visit the museum so there was no need for a ticket taker. I don't know how the museum's bills were paid but we are not talking hundreds of thousands of dollars."

"But the paperwork is still intact?"

"As far as I know. Ask Regina Hemmingway. Her company did the hauling of the museum property."

Noonan made a note to ask Regina Hemmingway about the file cabinets of management paperwork. "A few more questions."

"Go ahead."

"Are you sure all the artifacts were boxed and sent out? Are you sure none were left here at the bank?"

"Positive. It's not as if I was standing beside the men putting the artifacts into the boxes and crates, but I did have to authorize the shipments out. There was a dribble until there were six pallets worth. The final loading of the artifacts was on six pallets and was done at Chugach Shipping."

"So, no pallets, boxes, crates or envelopes with artifacts or provenances were hidden away or left here at the bank?"

"Not a one. As the museum rooms were being cleared, we were installing counters, desks, and executive lounge furniture. Every item of the museum that was here went. I signed for every load. I know."

CHAPTER 11

One of the curses of law enforcement, Noonan knew, was the lingering feeling that all was not copacetic. 'Copacetic' was not a word he often used for the simple reason most crimes – or actions which appeared to be crimes – came with evidence pointing in the direction the case would take — even for the cleverest crimes. Sooner or later, MOM was revealed. There was no *crime* until a court stated one had been committed. The heavy lifting of proving a *crime* was on the shoulders of the City, State and/or Federal attorneys but the evidence had to be collected in the field. It had to be clean and irrefutable. One mistake in the process, one slip-up, one misstep, and a bad guy or gal was going to walk.

The advantage the cop in the field had was, again, MOM: MOTIVE, OPPORTUNITY, and MEANS. It would be incredibly hard for a defendant to slip the bonds of justice if MOM was against him. Or her. Did he or she have a MOTIVE for the crime? Did he or she have the OPPORTUNITY to commit the crime? Finally, did he or she have the MEANS to commit the crime?

The specific problem Noonan faced with the disappearing of the artifacts was that MOM did not apply. There was no MOTIVE for someone to steal objects that had no street value. Even if there had been a MOTIVE, there appeared to be no OPPORTUNITY to steal the artifacts. The chain of supervision appeared unbroken. As there was neither MOTIVE nor OPPORTUNITY, MEANS was nonsensical.

This was all very well and good, as they say in the churches, but it still left a giant hole in the logical and rational universe. Something that no longer existed. An artifact might not have had a street value, but it had to have been *associated* with a street value; otherwise, the effort was wasted. That is, if the artifacts had no street value, why steal them? Something about the artifacts had to have a value, and a very large one for someone – or someones to – pull off the disappearing act. It was inconceivable that the artifacts would remain missing for a lengthy period of time. It was not as if they were the Amber Room valued at $500 million.

Something was very wrong here. Noonan could feel it in his bones. But what was it? He had all the facts before him. What was missing? What had he not been told?

Sitting at an empty table in the Loussac Library, he mentally spread out the facts as he knew them. But did he have all the facts? Was there a single artifact that was worth the entire charade? He needed to go over the artifact list carefully. Maybe there was something he was missing. But the problem was the people who could give him the answer were not trustworthy. It was not as if Harrison Anderson of the Aboriginal Artifact Commission would lie or that Regina Hemmingway had absconded with the artifacts. It was just that both were too close to the basic problem.

As any good cop does, Noonan listed the loose wires on the disappearing artifacts. First was the money trail. Did all of the money from the museum account actually make it to the Aboriginal Artifact Commission? Second, did the National Bank of Anchorage Museum really close? If it was still in existence on paper, someone could be collecting money for the defunct museum. Third, what about the pencil claimant, the fourth name on the nonprofit paperwork? Did he really have Alzheimer's, or was it a ploy? And if it was a ploy, what part did he play? And if he was a part of the scheme, was it possible the artifacts were hidden in the Senior Home for Pioneers where he was supposedly living? The last item was a v-e-r-y l-o-n-g shot. What about this

William Chambers person? A man from Boston opening a museum in Anchorage? What was his motive?

Tracing the existence of the nonprofit was easy. Noonan just pulled the IRS listing of nonprofits and found the National Bank of Anchorage Museum had closed. Or, at least, it had listed its demise two years earlier. The finances were listed as $5,789.15 which was in line with what Choi Walton had told him. The fourth name on the Board of Directors of the now-defunct museum nonprofit was Jerome Hemmingway. Noonan recognized the addresses for Harrison Anderson and the two Hemingway Board members as their places of business. He jotted down Jerome Hemmingway's address.

Then he placed a call to Choi Walton.

"Heinz! See I got it right! Calling a cop by his first name and being formal."

"Ah," Noonan said as he chuckled. "The joys of city living. I just have a few questions for you. I am hopeful I can get some answers without having to leap through hoops with the local police."

"I'll tell you what I can as long as," Walton was comical as she let her voice drift downward, "you never say you got the information from me."

"Of course," Noonan said in the saw low voice, "because we never talked."

They both laughed.

"OK," Walton was now in her normal voice, "what dastardly deed are you investigating?"

"Money," said Noonan dryly. "Always the money. When the National Bank of Anchorage Museum closed, it closed its account, correct?"

"Correct."

"Did it have more than one account?"

"Several. But don't get excited. It had one for the museum, itself. For its day-to-day operations. That's the one I closed out. It had a little more than $5,000. The museum had a second account, and it was for the personal use of the founder, William Chambers. It was a joint account, and it was closed by probate. When he died, the money went to family back in Boston."

"How much was in that account?"

"I can tell you because it went to probate. It's been a while, but I'd say it was about $15,000. Just in case you are getting all law and order on me, the check was written to a trust in Boston. I put it in the mail myself."

"How about the third account? You said several. Was there a third account?"

"Yes, and it is still open. Again, don't get excited. There's only about $5,000 in it. When William Chambers died, he was removed from the Board of Directors. The new Board was the four people I told you about. As soon as Chambers was gone, everyone knew the money he had been pumping into the museum was going to dry up. So, the new Board of Directors of the new nonprofit began a fundraising effort. Some donation checks were written to the museum, so they went into that account. As the fundraising continued, the checks were written to the Aboriginal Artifact Commission."

"Why hasn't that account been closed?"

"Probably because the amount is so small compared to the overall budget of the Commission. When it wants the money, we'll write a check."

"To the Commission?" Noonan hinted.

"Or the nonprofit. Their choice. No loose money, Heinz." She chortled as she said *Heinz*.

"Did the Aboriginal Artifact Commission open an account for its efforts at fundraising?"

"It already had one and it was huge. Still is. I can't tell you how large. Funds raised for the museum written to the Commission went into their overall account. How much I do not know but not enough to keep the museum open. The Commission is audited every year so you could find out how much money was actually raised." She paused, "But don't get your law and order hopes up. We are talking about Native artifacts and a failing museum. Those who gave money did it for publicity. No one believed the museum was going to survive."

CHAPTER 12

The information from Choi Walton was not what Noonan had hoped for. Money was always a motive for the crime but there wasn't a lot here — money or crime. His next step was easy, so to speak. He wanted to run the names of everyone involved through the National Crime Information Center, NCIC, computer.

But he was in Anchorage, not Sandersonville. It would have taken too much time to get the Sandersonville Police Department to inform the Anchorage Police Department that Noonan was authorized to do a search on NCIC. If and when he needed a more definitive search, he'd make an effort but, for the moment, he just needed a Q&D, 'Quick and Dirty' search. There were a handful of internet companies that offered immediate information for about $30. Some of them were free. Or 'free' until you wanted more detailed data. But, for $30, it was worth his time.

And he got zip when it came to the guilty.

Other than parking tickets, speeding tickets and one noise complaint, no name was linked to anything nefarious. The only two names which raised his eyebrows, but only slightly, were Jerome and Johnathan Hemmingway. Jerome had a gambling arrest in an after-hours joint in Spenard, a seedy section of Anchorage, three decades earlier. Johnathan Hemmingway had several citations for overloads. Regina

Hemmingway was clean as were Harrison Anderson, Choi Walton, and Bernice Whitcomb. As an outlier, he ran the names of the two men at the Anchorage Warehouse and Storage Facility, Alberto Mutofa and Giuseppe Abramowitz. There were a lot of 'Alberto Mutofas' listed as "A. Mutofa," "Al Mutofa," and "Albert Mutofa," all of different ages but no "Alberto." None of the crimes were serious, some DUIs and marijuana arrests when marijuana was not legal in Alaska. Abramowitz had some marijuana arrests as well but nothing else.

William Chambers was a cipher.

Rather, the Chambers family was a cipher.

When Noonan pulled up William Chambers on the internet he got, quite literally, six centuries of information. It was, in triplicate, a business, nonprofit and philanthropic family. The family emanated from John Chambers on the MAYFLOWER. He had six daughters who married well and produced descendants who were, to quote Wikipedia, "associated largely with both the 'Boston Brahmins' and Harvard's "intellectual aristocracy." Into the 21st Century, they had their fingers in all manner of pies: businesses, nonprofits, museums, multinationals, research institutions and travel enterprises. There were, quite literally, scads of "William Chambers," many of which could have been the Anchorage William Chambers.

When in doubt, you go back to the beginning and start again. So, Noonan called Choi Walton at the National Bank of Anchorage for the names of the associates of William Chambers in Boston. She didn't have a name, just a law firm, Chalmer and Chalmer.

Jedidiah Chalmer was charming.

For a lawyer.

"Alaska, right! Always wanted to go there." He paused, "In the summer."

"Good choice of seasons," Noonan chuckled as he opened his notebook. "I'm calling about the Chambers Museum here in Anchorage."

"Ah, the Chambers Museum. That's in the process of being closed out. I thought it would have happened by now but there were — are – some problems. Who are you again?"

"Heinz Noonan. I'm a police officer from Sandersonville, North Carolina on vacation. I was asked to help straighten things out."

"I don't know how I can help you very much. Chalmer and Chalmer handles many Chambers family matters. Without their permission I cannot discuss any of those matters. But I can discuss the museum because it is defunct. What is it you wanted to know?"

"Thanks for the help. Frankly, not much. Just some backup. Why was William Chambers in Alaska? I take it the rest of the family is in Boston."

"The extended family is all over the East Coast. They originated in Boston. Having a family member in a distant location is not unusual. The Chambers do have other holdings in Alaska, but they are not a museum."

"Really?"

"Yes. They do not carry the Chambers' name, the reason they did not pop on the State's dba list. Do you know what dba is?"

"'Doing business as.' What holdings do the Chambers still have in Alaska."

"It's public knowledge, so to speak, so I can discuss them. There are some percentages in hunting lodges, minority partners in corporations that do business in Alaska, some copper holdings that are not being worked, and investments in some construction and shipping companies. But we are talking low percentages."

"How low?"

"Oh, no more than 30%. That's for the lodges. For some of the larger businesses, the holdings are in stock rather than percentages. They also have mutual funds which invest in companies that may have an Alaskan connection."

"Do they have any holdings in Chugach Shipping?"

"Not the way you mean it. I know that Chugach Shipping, or at least the owners, are partners in a nonprofit that are liquidating the National Bank of Anchorage Museum. So, no, the Chambers have no financial connection to Chugach Shipping, the business, but, yes, the Chambers do have personal financial connections to the owners."

"Have you been in touch with those individuals?"

"Lately or last year?"

"Lately."

There was a sigh on the phone and then the reply. "Off and on. Closing the museum has been very difficult for the Chambers family."

"Oh? Why?" Noonan asked.

"It's not as if the museum was a business. When you have a business and you want to close it, you just pay the bills, lock the door, and turn in the key to the landlord. That can't be done with a museum. The artifacts must be cataloged and packed for their ultimate destination. The museum paperwork has to be maintained in one location so if the IRS wants proof that someone donated to the museum in, say, five years, the paperwork still exists. There are insurance problems if the artifacts are damaged during transport to the new locations. I know the artifacts are missing because I was called by the insurance woman who works with the Aboriginal Artifact Commission. And I speak with Harrison Anderson of the Commission frequently."

"About what?"

"Mostly financial matters. But the only link I and the Chambers family have with him at this point is financial. We had to work out the details of closing the books of the museum. Family details I cannot discuss. Let's just say that when Mr. Chambers died, his personal money was returned to the family. Museum money that came through Mr. Chambers, went to the nonprofit."

Somewhere in the depths of Noonan's cerebral cortex, a distant gong chimed.

"How much museum money are we talking about?"

"Not millions. I can't tell you the exact amount. But the family money dried up. The nonprofit did extensive fundraising, but it was not adequate to keep the museum open."

Again, Noonan heard the chime.

"So, there was some money from the family that continued to flow into the museum?"

"*Through* the family. Some of the family money for the museum came from bequests or trusteeships. For instance, if a family member left the museum $5,000 a year as part of an inheritance, the money would automatically be sent to the museum. That money would not stop until the trustees of the inheritance voted to stop the payments. For some of these families, $5,000 is such a small amount it would not warrant a meeting of the Board of Trustees."

Noonan chose his words carefully. "There is an account with the National Bank of Anchorage for William Chambers that is still open. Is that where that inheritance money would go?"

"Yes. But we are playing a vocabulary game. If a will says to leave $10,000 to Will Chambers for his Anchorage Museum, the money goes to Will Chambers's account in Anchorage because there is no Anchorage Museum account. Until all the artifacts are safe and sound in their new home, that account must stay open."

"Are any other dollars expected to go that that account?"

"Not sure. But again, not hundreds of thousands of dollars."

"But any other money that are donated to the museum from the family would end up in that account?"

"If a will or testament or whatever legal instrument might state the money should be to William Chambers or, for that matter, to the nonprofit that tried to save the museum, yes."

"But if it does *not* mention the museum, where would the money go?"

"Wherever the trustees or executors or the Board of the probate account want it to go."

"When the account is finally closed, where will the money go?"

"Legally, the money was for the museum so it would go to the museum. But since there is no museum, it would go to the nonprofit. But since the nonprofit has been disbanded and the artifacts are scattered, any money would probably go to the Aboriginal Artifact Commission."

CHAPTER 13

Money.

Crime and money.

When it comes to crime, there are five motivating factors: greed, anger, jealously, revenge, or pride. This is good news, so to speak, for law enforcement, because it gives the detective a start. One by one, he or she, eliminates one factor after another. In Noonan's case, he did see any anger, jealousy, pride, or revenge as a motivating factor for the disappearing of the artifacts. Greed was all that was left. But greed meant money and artifacts had no financial value on the street. So, what was he missing? The artifacts did not vanish by themselves. There was human action involved. Lost was possible but highly unlikely.

But where was the money?

It appeared that every dime had been tracked so, what ....?

Noonan was playing with scenarios – none of which were worthy of serious consideration – while he was drinking his first cup of coffee of the morning in the Loussac Library mezzanine when Bernice Whitcomb sat down at his table with a binder of paperwork.

"I was pretty sure you don't have access to a computer other than the one here in the library, so I copied everything I had. Sorry, but I don't think you'll find much of what you are looking for. Or think you know what you are looking for. These," she indicated the files, "are just a list of the artifacts, who donated them, when, and where they are going once the load shows up. The dollar figures are simply pie-in-the-sky. Those are just to give the home office an idea of the kind of money we are talking about."

Noonan pawed through the paperwork for a few moments. "Correct me if I'm wrong, but if the artifacts are not found and your company has to pay for the loss, the checks will go to the museums where the artifacts were supposed to be delivered."

"Yes. Some of the money will go to the Aboriginal Artifact Commission for its expenses. Which will include Chugach Shipping. But we are not talking very much." Noonan started to speak but she cut him off. "I know, I know. The cop in you is looking for the big bucks. Well, there aren't any here. The Aboriginal Artifact Commission is going to get about $15,000 from the nonprofit and that will include about $10,000 for Chugach Shipping. I think Chugach Shipping has already been paid so I guess that means the Commission will get that whole ball of wax." She twirled the index finger of her right hand in the air as a sign of 'whoopee!'

"So, there's not a lot of cash at your end of this affair."

"$25,000 which, to the Commission, is chicken feed."

"So where are the big dollars?" Noonan said to himself as Whitcomb went for a cup of coffee.

When Whitcomb came back, she gave Noonan an odd look. "Are you really called the 'Bearded Holmes?'"

"I don't call me that. I'm just Heinz."

"According to the police here in town, you are pretty good at odd things. Crimes and all."

"I've been lucky."

"But you specialize in the unusual."

"I don't specialize in anything. People just call with odd circumstances, and I do what I can."

"Do you charge?"

Noonan gave her an odd look. "Not really. Let me guess; you've got an odd problem."

Whitcomb gave a 'who me?' look. Then she said, "Well, yeah. But I'm not a cop and what happened is not a crime. At least not as far as I know."

Noonan gave a wry smile and shook his head. "Well, let's hear it. Maybe I can help."

"It's unusual. Even for someone like me who's been in the insurance business for quite a while."

Noonan wiggled the index finger of his right hand in the 'give it to me' indicator.

"It's odd. Someone stole a section of a staircase from the Municipal Hospital. No one knows why. I mean, why would anyone steal a section of a staircase?"

"Well," Noonan said. "It is odd. I'll give you that. Are we talking about a staircase like in GONE WITH THE WIND of a collection of stairs that had yet to be installed or screwed into place?"

"Because of the configuration of the building, the staircase, the whole one, must do an odd half-circle next to the elevator shaft. The elevator is being expanded as well. Doubling from one to two. The staircase must wind its way up from the bottom floor to the main floor around the elevator shaft."

"If there are stairs, why an elevator?"

"Wheelchairs primarily. There are two entrances to the hospital. The old one, being renovated, is the west entrance next to the old Emergency Room. The new, expanded Emergency Room is being relocated at the east entrance. The hospital was built into a slope, so the east entrance is three floors above the west entrance. This means patients with wheel-chairs entering from the parking lot on the west have to take the elevator up to the Emergency Room. The west entrance has been around for a while, but it is – or was – hard for patients to use. I guess you'd say it was more of a service entrance. So, the decision was made to upgrade it. That entrance leads to a gallery that is about three floors lower than the main entrance on the east side. By that, I mean when you enter on the west side, you are looking up a ceiling, say, 60 feet up. But there are hospital rooms on all three sides of the west entryway. It's ingrained wood – or will be ingrained wood – when the project is complete."

Noonan opened up his notebook.

"So, you'll help me?"

"Why not? Keep talking."

"Thanks, Heinz. This is an odd one."

"All my loo-loo cases are odd. Now, let me tell you what you told me and when I go wrong, let me know."

"Fine."

Noonan looked at his notes. "A hospital wants its patients on wheelchairs to come in the east entrance where the Emergency Room is now located. But patients are still coming through the west entrance which is three floors lower than the entrance on the east. The west entryway is kind of like an artistic shaft with no hospital corridor entrances. There is, right now, one elevator shaft which the hospital is increasing to two."

Whitcomb cut in. "The elevator shaft has already been expanded to two. The old one goes to every floor. The new elevator is high speed and begins at the east entrance and goes to certain floors. Primarily operating rooms. Patients can use the high-speed elevators when they are not being used in an emergency."

"So, the high-speed elevator is the new one?"

"Right. It starts from the mezzanine floor on the east side of the building."

"And the high-speed elevator is only accessible from the mezzanine on the east side of the building?"

"Yes. Patients coming in the west entrance have to use the old elevator."

"Now, the stairs."

"There was a narrow stairway in the original building, but it is not used by that many patients."

Noonan tapped his notebook. "Because most patients were coming in the east entrance."

"Yes. But with the expansion of the hospital – federal funds and all – there is a major renovation and all of the material is coming in the west entrance. Everything was pulled out and the western wall was partially removed so all of the construction crews, equipment and material could get in. The old staircase was removed and bracing for the new one was put in. It is a much wider staircase with snazzy handrails."

"And this is the one that's missing?" Noonan asked.

"A section of it. The staircase has six parts, so to speak, landings, actually. The staircase kind of winds around the walls and the elevator shaft. Or, now, shafts. I mean, we are talking about a three-story climb from the west entrance to the mezzanine."

"So, the staircase will be secured to the walls rather than up the center of the entranceway?"

"It has to be. Otherwise, a patient in a wheelchair would have to wiggle around going up the staircase."

"Is the west entryway being used now?"

"By patients, not that much. It has piles of material and some smaller cranes and, you know, construction equipment. A beehive. Patients can use the entrance, but it is a chore dodging the piles of materials and workers. There is quite a bit of dust in the air and debris on the floor." She paused, "So the staircase was delivered in sections. Six of them."

"And the staircase sections were unloaded in the entryway area?" Noonan asked.

"Yes. The six sections were signed in. Or delivered. I have the paperwork."

"Then one was stolen?" Noonan asked as he was writing in his notebook.

"Not yet," Whitcomb sighed. "The framing was put in for the staircase steps, all six of them. Five were put in. 'In' as in bolted to the frames. The sixth one was put in place and was expected to be bolted in the next day. That would have finished the walkway. But the next morning, the stairs were gone."

Noonan fiddled with his pen. "'Gone' as in removed and placed on the floor of the Hospital entryway or 'gone,' as in stolen?"

"I don't want to use the word 'stolen' just yet. But it was 'gone' as in not on the frame to be bolted in and not on the entryway floor. It stalled construction until another stairway section could be found."

"That is odd," Noonan said as he wrote in his notebook. "And the stairway section was never found?"

"Gone and never found."

"Interesting. At the very least. When did this happen?"

"About three weeks ago," Whitcomb said flatly. "About the same time the artifacts disappeared."

A gong sounded in the deepest recess of Noonan's cerebellum.

"Huh. Odd. Any connection to the artifacts?"

"Actually, yes. That's why I'm talking to you."

"Do tell."

"The name of the company that was responsible for bringing in the new staircase section was Chugach Shipping."

CHAPTER 14

The Anchorage Memorial Hospital was a composite structure. This description was very Alaskan. It was also typical of Anchorage. Because of geography and the United States military, the city of Anchorage is exceedingly small in terms of acres when compared to other cities its size in the Lower 48. It is triangular with two sides running along the shoreline of Cook Inlet. The third side is Joint Base Elmendorf Fort Richardson, JBER for short. JBER was initially an Army base with an Army Air Corp extension. On September 26, 1947, when the United States Secretary of Defense created the United States Air Force, overnight the Army Air Corps on Fort Richardson became Elmendorf Air Force Base. In 2005, they were geographically rejoined.

Generally speaking, Anchorage is a massive triangle. The north end of the city is pinched off by the Anchorage Port on the waterfront, and inland by JBER. The shoreline wanders south for about 60 blocks. Here the city is at its deepest, 85 blocks from the waterfront to JBER at the back of town. From there to the south end of town, at about 120 blocks, where the city pinches off by the highway headed south. There are homes scattered on the western slope of the Chugach Mountains but the business district, including the four hospitals, is 40 blocks in width. What this means to someone from the Lower 48 is 90% of the city can be seen from the top of any of the city's skyscrapers – all of them under 25 stories.

Further, this means every square foot within city limits has a use. Even the vacant lots. During the summer they are a nuisance, but during the winter they are where snow is piled up after it has been plowed off the streets.

The Anchorage Municipal Hospital is a composite structure because it has seven high-rise medical business structures on the same property along with ten floors of the traditional hospital. These high-rise structures have doctors' offices, minor surgery operations, dental clinics, pharmacies, and an indoor playground/childcare for both medical staff and patients. Immediately behind the hospital is a small, regional airport. This is critical to bush residents because it means access to the hospital is just a walk from the landing strip rather than an expensive emergency vehicle delivery across the city. Because it serves the bush, those areas of Alaska which are not connected to the Lower 48 states with a road, the hospital has a reputation for high-quality telemedicine services. Further, it is close to inexpensive motels so bush residents do not have to be pay for taxi service between the hospital and where they spend the night.

The popularity of the hospital did not come without a cost. Because of that popularity, the hospital was constantly in upgrade, both technologically and physically. The technological upgrades were like those in all parts of the country. Medical treatment was jet streaming into the future and the equipment that had been standard a year ago was suddenly only fit for cavepeople. This was an ongoing expense, but it meant better medical care for every ailment and surgical need.

On the flip side, it meant constant upgrading of the physical structure. The wiring which had been installed when the hospital was constructed was no longer adequate. Operating rooms were too small for the addition of new equipment. Utility services were 'growingly inadequate' for the influx of patients and technological advances and the pharmacy had gone from a one-person operation from 9 to 5 to a 24/7 service.

The most visible upgrade Noonan saw was the expansion of the western entrance to the structure. While it was supposedly closed to the public, there was no way of knowing it. The entry was jam-packed with piles of construction material and equipment around which queues of patients formed a trail, some with walkers and others in wheelchairs.

"It's like a great railway terminal but without the rails," Noonan said to Whitcomb. "I'm surprised there haven't been any accidents."

"Welcome to Alaska, Heinz. Even in our largest city," Whitcomb raised her right hand to indicate Anchorage, "we're still small compared to Seattle, Los Angeles, or Atlanta. By Lower 48 standards, we're rural."

Noonan laughed. "That's what people say about Sandersonville. Now," he pointed to the staircase that was flush against the wall, "that's the staircase that had the missing section."

"You got it. This entryway," she pointed to the cathedral-like room, "was designed to be the original entrance. But there was a problem." She pointed to a coffee shop nestled against the elevator shaft. "Originally, before Anchorage got big, the coffee shop was the check in. It didn't have to be large because Anchorage wasn't that big. That was before the Trans-Alaska boomtime. In the 1970s. This hospital was built for the locals and the people who flew in from the bush. That's why the hospital is located close to the landing strip." She pointed to the west. "Everything was small then because there was no reason it had to be big. Then came the Pipeline Boom and everything had to get big. Come here." She guided Noonan alongside the coffee shop to a narrow hallway.

"Originally, this was the entrance to hospital. Patients would check in at the desk where the coffee shop is now. Then they would walk around – or ride in the wheelchairs – down this hallway to what is the ground floor on this side of the hospital. The hospital is built into the side of a hill so there is also a ground floor on the east side of the building," She pointed upwards. "But that has all changed. See, originally, the Emergency Room was down here. On the ground floor of the West Entrance, where we are now." She pointed to doors that ran along a hallway which extended in both directions behind the elevator shaft and coffeeshop.

"So, this was the original Emergency Room?" Noonan asked.

"Yup, before it was moved upstairs. You came in this entrance, the west one, so you can see how congested it could get with ambulances and patients in wheelchairs or in walkers. When the Pipeline Boom came, the hospital had to be expanded. So, the Emergency Room was moved upstairs. Not really 'upstairs,'" she made quotes in the air with her fingers, "because the hospital is built into a hill. On the east side," she pointed upwards, "The ground floor on the east side is a floor above us. Actually, a bit more. I'd say 20 or 25 feet. But it doesn't matter. There are three floors here at the western entrance and the rest of the hospital is above. This," she pointed to the hallway, "is the first floor on the elevators. Floor Three is the ground entrance on the eastern side of the building. That's the entrance for the new elevator."

Noonan backed up and looked at the cathedral ceiling. "This is quite impressive. I mean, we are talking about a hospital. Every hospital I have ever visited, the space emphasis has been on hospital rooms and labs and pharmacies."

"Welcome to Alaska. We have to be all things to all people. Now," she pointed to the staircase plastered against the wall. "That's the staircase you are interested in. It was installed as a walkway so the elevator could be used exclusively by wheelchair and walker patients."

"And gurneys?"

"Yeah. Before the east entrance was built, this," she pointed to the doorway to the west entrance, "was the entrance to the Emergency Room."

Noonan pointed down the hall they had just left. "So, the Emergency Room, the original one, was down that hall?"

"Correct. Then, when the new Emergency Room came online upstairs, the old Emergency Room was turned into hospital rooms. Generally speaking, and I know because I was a party of the discussions, rather, my company was, the operating rooms are on the ground floor, the eastern entrance ground floor, and the floor above it. The renovation of the hospital was done that way, so the new elevator starts at the ground floor on the eastern entrance. Patients coming in here, through the western entrance, now, only need to take the elevator to the check-in counter on the east entrance ground floor upstairs. The emergency patients are no longer entering here so the elevator renovation is not needed here."

Noonan walked over to a pile of particle board. "What you are telling me is the bulk of the renovation is upstairs from here. Other than the staircase," he pointed to the winding staircase against the wall of the cathedral-like room, "no construction is being done down here."

"I can't give you a solid 'yes or no.' All of the rooms down here," she pointed down the hallway, "were changed from the old Emergency Room to the hospital rooms and that coffee shop," she pointed to the coffee shop, "was the old check-in. But that was a while ago. My guess is the elevator mechanism for the new elevator," she pointed to the expansion of the elevator shaft, "is down here. On the ground floor down here. It makes more sense than digging down to install the mechanism. And there's probably some reinforcing of the structure's walls down here. I don't know. But I do know who to ask."

CHAPTER 15

Clarence Ivanakof could have played for any position on the front line of any NFL team. "Thought about it," he said when Noonan asked if he ever played football, "but I wanted a career that would last, not one that vanished with the first solid hit. Had enough of them in high school."

"Good choice," Noonan said. "Now, what can you tell me about the western entrance that I don't already know?"

Ivankof laughed. "Not much to tell that you can't see. All of the construction work is upstairs. Down here," he pointed to the elevator shaft, "the only significant work is the elevator shaft. The new elevator does not come all the way down here, but we still need the support of the ground to stabilize the shaft. The new shaft. The old shaft is doing fine. It's been checked over the years and is holding up just fine."

Noonan scratched his head. "Alaska is famous for permafrost. I know because I have in-laws up here. Permafrost is permanently frozen ground but that 'permanently' is not that permanent if something is built over it. Several of my in-laws have sump pumps for their basement crawl spaces. Is there permafrost under the Hospital?"

Ivankof gave a sad smile. "Tough question. Yes, permafrost is permanently frozen soil.

But the terms 'permanent' and 'frozen' are misleading. Permafrost in the Arctic, yes, is permanent and frozen. Except around the drilling platforms, roads, and structures. But the further south you go, the less 'permanent' and 'frozen' the soil is. Down here, in Anchorage, the permafrost is most appropriately described as lenses. In some areas there is thick permafrost, others none at all. In between could be a mix. When it comes to permafrost in Anchorage, nothing is for sure. On top of that, you have new construction and global climate change which affects the soil. What I am saying is you raise a fine point. The answer is iffy. All of the inspections of the existing elevator shaft and, for that matter, the footings of the hospital have shown no displacement. But then, the footing for the original structure was deep into the soil. Deep into the permafrost when it was present. That doesn't mean things won't change, but it does mean, in answer to your question, the elevator shafts can carry the weight."

"Will the new shafts change anything down here?" Noonan asked as he indicated the western entrance.

"Not really. As you can see, the work on the new shaft is done. The lift mechanism has been installed so there's nothing else to be done, construction wise." He pointed to the piles of construction material on the west entrance ground floor. "What you see here are for two more floors of the hospital and renovations of the existing rooms and surgery center. But this material is misleading because what you see here are just the easy parts of the expansion. The surgery centers, on two floors, are going to need a lot of wiring and plumbing for the new equipment. Surgery rooms are not just oversized hospital rooms. Modern equipment is bulky and needs a lot of power."

"Where's the power going to come from?"

"The easy answer is the municipal grid. The hospital has half a floor of backup generators, and it also has a bank of solar panels. The solar panels are 24/7, of course, and if there is a massive, long-term power failure, the solar power is direct and parceled on a priority basis, surgery rooms first so on and so forth."

Noonan smiled. "Well, thanks for the overview, I'm primarily interested in the western entrance. I was told you had a missing section of the staircase."

Ivankof smiled. "I was told of that. We get mix-ups all the time."

"What exactly was missing?"

Ivankof pointed to a section of the staircase. "The staircase, that one, was being re-installed along the wall. The original staircase was old and rutted so it was removed and a new one installed. We used the same format but with new bolts and stairs. Everything appeared to be going well and one morning we found a section of the staircase missing."

"The bracings too?"

"No, just the steps. The bracings were still in place, just the steps."

"The bolts too?"

"Yeah. We guessed that there was some kind of a flaw in the steps." He looked at Whitcomb, "We're prescient. If something looks like a problem, we solve it right away. My bet, someone saw a problem with the stairs, the steps, and said, 'Let's not take a chance,' and removed them."

"No one said anything to you?" Noonan asked.

"No reason to. That's a ground-level decision. Besides, no one is going to admit they went off the reservation on a hunch. Besides, the cost of the new stairs is not even chicken feed for a project this size. No, someone saw a problem with the steps and fixed it. Kudos to them."

CHAPTER 16

Jerome Hemmingway was amiable but gave every indication he was a lost soul. But then again, that's what Alzheimer's does. You are still operational in the sense you have a normal existence, but when it comes to the past, it is gone.

Noonan and Whitcomb paid a visit to Hemmingway at the Senior Home for Alaska Pioneers in downtown Anchorage. There was no question he should be a resident of the home. He was in his 90s and looked it. He was quite thin, had pasty hair cut short, walked with a cane and had a weak handshake. But he was ambulatory and was an amiable sort. His room was sparse when it came to furniture, but he had a special chair and light for reading in a corner. There was a full bookshelf along one wall next to the doorway. The walls with no doorways were plastered with photographs, none of them framed. The third wall was a sliding glass door leading to a balcony. There was a large potted plant on the unmovable side of the doorway. A battered couch stretched along one wall and there was an easy chair in the center of the room. There were piles of newspapers and magazines alongside the easy chair and a large screen for the television on a stand to the side of the chair. A pair of reading glasses were on a small table between the easy chair and the large screen.

The three shared pleasantries and Jerome indicated Noonan and Whitcomb should sit on the couch. The two sat and then Noonan asked how he was related to Regina and Johnathan Hemmingway.

"I don't know them," Hemming replied as he pinched his eyes as though he was struggling to recall the names. "Where do I know you from?" he said to Noonan. And then to Whitcomb, "I don't know you either. I mean, I don't remember you. Where did we meet?"

"We've never met," Whitcomb was pleasant. "We're here to talk about the National Bank of Anchorage Museum."

"A museum? What museum? Here in town?"

"You were on the Board of the museum. Do you remember that?"

"No. Where do I know you from?"

Now Noonan took the lead. He pointed to the bookshelf. "You've done quite a bit of reading, Jerome. Where did you get all those books?"

"Books? Oh, those books. I collected them, I guess. Tell me again, where do I know you from?"

"You don't, Jerome. We've never met. We just wanted to have a talk with you about Regina and Johnathan. They're your niece and nephew, right?"

"Regina and Johnathan," he said as he squinted his eyes. "No, no, I don't know them. Should I know them?"

"Probably your brother's or sister's children. Did you have a brother or sister?"

"Must have if I have nieces and nephews. Who are you again?"

"Bernice Whitcomb. But we've never met."

"Well, that's why I don't remember you."

"Do you remember Regina and Johnathan?"

"No, who are they?"

"Your niece and nephew."

"Do I have a niece and a nephew?"

"They say you are their uncle."

"How can I be their uncle if I have no children."

Whitcomb would not give up. "They are not your children. They are the children of your brother or sister."

"I don't have a brother or a sister."

Then she tried a different tack. Whitcomb pulled a document out of her handbag. "This is the nonprofit filing for the National Bank of Anchorage Museum. There's your signature. Do you remember signing this document?"

Hemming spent a few seconds looking at the signature. "It could be my signature."

"Do you remember signing this document?"

"What is the document?"

"Forming a nonprofit for the National Bank of Anchorage Museum. Last April."

"Is that my signature?" He looked at Whitcomb with a blank stare, "Where do I know you from?"

Whitcomb looked at Noonan for assistance. Again, Noonan took an obtuse tack. He rose from the couch and went to the bookshelf. "You must be quite a reader," Noonan said as he pulled a book from the shelf. "Law and all. Were you a lawyer?"

"Oh, yes. A fine lawyer. Made a living at it. Who are you again?"

"Heinz Noonan. We've never met." Noonan pointed to the shelf of books. "Not a lot of art books or mysteries. Do you read these books frequently?"

"Oh, yes, all the time. I was a lawyer once. Were you a client?"

"No, Mr. Hemming, I was never a client. Do you remember any clients?"

"I had a lot of clients. Were you one of them?"

At this point Whitcomb rose and stepped toward Jerome Hemmingway. She offered him her hand and he shook it. "It was nice meeting you, Mr. Hemming, maybe we'll meet again sometime."

Hemming gave a feeble shake. Noonan replaced the law book on the shelf and stepped to the back of Hemmingway's chair. He extended his hand alongside the right-hand armrest and tapped the older man's right hand. "It was nice seeing you, Mr. Hemming. We'll let ourselves out."

Hemming half turned and said, "Nice to see you two. Maybe we'll meet again."

Whitcomb and Noonan exited Hemming's room and walked down the hall. Whitcomb started to speak but Noonan stopped her by putting his index finger to his own lips. Whitcomb gave him an odd look but stopped talking. The two walked down the hallway to the elevator. When Whitcomb started to speak again, Noonan, again, silenced her with his right index finger.

On the main floor, Noonan stopped at the front desk. The attendant was all smiles. She was also very young. Her name tag read "Abigail" with no last name.

When she looked up, Noonan said, "Hi, Abigail, how you doin'?"

"Fine. How can I help you?"

"We just finished seeing Mr. Hemming. Up on the second floor."

"Isn't he a pleasant man. It's hard to believe he's in his 90s. Ooops, I'm not supposed to tell you that."

"Not a problem," Noonan said. "We'd," he pointed to himself and Whitcomb, "like to get him a subscription to *Alaska Magazine*. Is that all right?"

"Certainly. I'm sure he'll like the reading material."

"Fine, fine. When the magazine comes, tell him it's from his nephew and niece, Regina and Johnathan. Mr. Hemming doesn't know us," again Noonan pointed at himself and Whitcomb. "We don't want him to think the subscription was a mistake."

"I'm sure they'll be pleased. I'll tell Johnathan when he comes in on Tuesday."

CHAPTER 17

Noonan kept Whitcomb silent until they made it back to her car a block away from the entrance to the Senior Home for Alaska Pioneers. When they were both in the car, Whitcomb turned to Noonan and said, "What, exactly, went on back there?"

"He's a con," Noonan said offhandedly. "A very good con. A fine actor too. He's sharp as a tack. Hasn't lost a single brain cell in 90 years. He's the mastermind behind whatever is going on."

"How do you know that? I mean, I saw the same thing you did. I found him to be a befuddled old man."

"Hoodwinked you, he did!" Noonan said with humor in his voice. "Jerome Hemming is an extremely devious man. And a fine actor. Why shouldn't he be? He's got an entire four floors of seniors, many of whom have Alzheimer's. Or Dementia. He has plenty of real-world examples to copy."

"Maybe. But how did you know he was a con?"

"Oh, many things. Strongest were the books on the shelf. All law books. And all on the same subject: estates. Second, the pictures on his wall. They are all of different people. My bet, he got them from other residents when they passed or as gifts. None of the pictures were framed, just stuck on the wall. It's all part of the scam."

"What scam?" Whitcombe was clearly still trying to make sense of what Noonan was saying.

"That, Ms Whitcomb, is a very good question. And quite convoluted. See, the way I understand it, to be a resident of the Senior Home for Alaska Pioneers, you cannot have assets. That is, to be a resident you must have given all your money away. Or maybe you have no money. I know because I have some in-laws who will not go to the Senior Home for Alaska Pioneers because they do not want to give up their money. They don't have much, but they do have a home that is paid off. They can't give the house to their kids, because their kids have homes of their own and there is a lot of memorabilia they do not want to part with. So, they have taken going to the Senior Home for Alaska Pioneers off the table."

Whitcomb shook her head. "I don't know about that but, frankly, Mr. Hemming doesn't need much. He's got a warm home, three meals a day, and a room. What's he need money for?"

Noonan rolled his head back and forth. "Stop thinking about what is normal. We are up to our eyebrows in a sea of the unexplained. Why would anyone steal museum artifacts that have no value? Why would anyone steal a perfectly acceptable part of a staircase? Why is a 90-year-old lawyer faking dementia? My experience tells me there is money in this somehow, somewhere."

Whitcomb shook her head. "I don't see it."

Noonan squinted one eye as he looked at Whitcomb. "Believe me; it's there. What we have here is an exceedingly clever man. Rather, an exceedingly clever lawyer. Why does he want the money? Maybe he doesn't care. It might be just the game. Not so much one last hurrah but a way to stick it to the system one more time. He is the master manipulator. We are dealing with an incredibly clever man and time, so to speak, is on his side. And even if we can catch him, the courts are so slow he'll be laughing at us from his grave."

CHAPTER 18

The next day was Sunday and Noonan, along with his wife and the gaggle of in-laws scattered across Anchorage to their denomination of choice. Noonan and his wife were not churchgoing in the sense they set aside every Sunday morning for church service, but they were occasional in their attendance. They avoided church service on religious holidays because of the crush of Sunday Christians – and Unitarians – but preferred to donate their time and energy to social projects. Noonan's first choice was always finding moneys and food for free breakfast and lunches for school children and had no problem if their parents were partaking of the food stuffs.

But in Anchorage, it was church attendance with the in-laws. Because there were so many, attendance at any one particular church was not possible. But a mass attendance, so to speak, at lunch brought the scattered family together. Thereafter, the family scattered again for religious youth services, athletic workouts, homework completion and other social gatherings in which Noonan and his wife had no interest whatsoever. So, when the last of the French fries and burgers had been devoured, Noonan and his wife bid the gaggle *adieu* with the excuse they were returning home for a nap. This may have been an accurate statement for his wife, but when Noonan asked for his room key, the attendant pointed to a man sitting in the lobby.

"He's been waiting for you," the attendant said as he handed Noonan a note.

Noonan nodded to the man in the lobby as he looked at the note. Then he had to reread it. It simply read, "Why are the pyramids in Egypt?"

Noonan flipped the note over to see if there was anything written on the back of the note. Nothing was.

When he approached, the man extended his right hand. "Jaron Flint. I'm the curator of the Anchorage Numismatic Museum and Emporium."

Noonan shook his hand. "That's odd," Noonan said as he squinted. "A museum and an emporium? Isn't that like two opposites in one location?"

Flint smirked. "Yes and no."

"I hate answers like that."

"As I am sure you are discovering, there is no money in a museum. This is why most museums, at least the ones in Anchorage, are partially government funding. If you have a private museum, like mine, it is very expensive. So, in my case, I have combined my store with a museum. The museum is a nonprofit so I can take donations but to keep the lights on the security system active, I use the profits from the store."

Noonan kind of nodded and then showed Flint the note. "This is from you?"

"Absolutely. You're the 'Bearded Holmes' guy from North Carolina. If I talked crime on Sunday, well, you might want to wave me off."

"Sundays are a day of rest. But now that you're here," Noonan waved the note. "Why are there pyramids in Egypt?"

"Because they are too heavy to be in the British Museum."

Noonan chortled. "Well, you have my attention now. What can do for the Flint Museum?"

"Works for me. Let's sit down," he indicated twin easy chairs in the hotel lobby. "Before I start, I need to ask if you know what scrip is?"

"I don't," Noonan said as he sat in the leather chair in the lobby. "I don't have a notebook with me so keep it simple so I can remember everything."

Flint laughed. "It is simple, so I'll keep it that way. Unfortunately, it will require a bit of a history lecture."

"I'm all ears."

"Again, keeping this as simple as possible, money does not exist. If you have $1,000 in your checking account and you go to your bank and ask to see your $1,000, the teller will laugh hysterically. You will be told your specific $1,000 does not exist. Your $1,000 is just an electronic blip.

"Now you can take $100 of that electronic blip in the form of paper. But that $100 bill is just paper. It has no value. What gives it *value* is the faith a grocery store, nightclub or restaurant has in that piece of paper. As long as everyone has faith in that $100 bill, it is worth $100 in goods and/or services."

"That's pretty basic," Noonan said.

"I agree," Flint continued. "For 99% of Americans, this is basic economics. You either have money or you do not, the old division of society, the haves and have-nots. But when it comes to cash, today, people do not have that much. Rare is the person who buys goods and services with cash. Most of us use checks or credit cards. Many of us pay our bills with automatic withdrawals or, for larger items like cars, boats, or houses, we simply 'sign our life away' on sheets of paper – one signature or initial at a time. Cash, the way we know it, has only been standard since 1933. Before 1933, the saga of the American dollar was twisted, bizarre and unbelievably complex. Can I go on?"

"Please do."

"Before the American Revolution, by and large, the colonists used the English Pound as the American currency. But after the French and Indian War, when the British government began taxing and overtaxing the colonies, a lot of Americans began using the Spanish dollar. This was because more and more goods were being smuggled into the colonies from the Caribbean. The Spanish dollar was also convenient because he had 100 parts, pennies, to make a dollar. After the American Revolution, there was a wide variety of things used as currency including whiskey. The United States Constitution did not establish a currency, but it left that power to the states. The states allowed banks to print the money.

"What usually happened was someone deposited money in a bank, say $1,000, and then the banks allowed the individual to withdraw small amounts in the form of bank notes. The Bank of New York would print Bank of New York dollars which were as good as the Bank of New York.

And that was the problem. If the Bank of New York went under, everyone who had money in that bank lost everything. Just as bad, the Bank of the New York dollars were only good in those stores and restaurants that accepted Bank of New York dollars. You could buy a ham sandwich from a restaurant across the street from the Bank of New York but in what is now Queens, Brooklyn or Baltimore, Bank of New York dollars were just paper. If you wanted to use your banked money outside of New York, you usually took gold. Gold was accepted everywhere. But no one walked around with pockets of gold. That was foolhardy.

"Things, monetarily speaking, became quite complicated in the 1820s with the expanded use of the steam engine. Suddenly there were trains chugging across state lines and steamships plying the Mississippi River and all its tributaries. Some kind of uniform currency was needed but there was no legal mechanism to make it happen. People were very skeptical about 'new' banks and preferred to leave their money in banks that had longevity. One of the tried and true, dependable banks was the Citizens Bank of Louisiana. Everyone knew money in *that* bank was sound – and spendable in many cities. Since Louisiana had both English and French-speaking residents, their currency had French on one side and English on the other. The ten-dollar bill had "ten dollars" on the English side and, on the French side, "Dix" for ten. This was the origin of the term Dixieland."

"I did not know that," Noonan said with interest. "I'm always interested in bits of history I did not know before."

Flint continued. "Nothing much changed until the Civil War. Then it was the 'Tale of Two Currencies.' One was simple, the other – on its best days – convoluted. The tale of Union money is easiest. The United States Army was all over the map, so to speak, so it was necessary to have a currency that was good all over that same map. If there was a United States Army unit in Pittsburg, the vendors in Pittsburg were not going to accept dollars printed by a bank in Philadelphia or New York. So, the United States government, in this case, the North, the Union, began printing what we now call United States dollars. They were printed on green paper and immediately became known as 'greenbacks.' The term survives to this day. What made the greenbacks acceptable was they were backed with gold. This was the start of gold being used to 'back up' United States dollars.

"But there were not that many greenbacks in circulation and the money was primarily used by the United States government for large vendors. So, by and large, bank-printed money was still used for everyday purchases. Where the bank was located, the city, its notes were accepted as currency.

"In actuality, there were many forms of *currency* being used. This was out of necessity. Before the Civil War started, there was not much need for 'things.' But as soon as the war started, there was an instantaneous need for many 'things.' For the North, it was an overnight industrialization boom. An army in the field needed food, boots, guns, bullets, cannons, and uniforms. Those 'things' had to be transported by wagons, initially, and then railroads. The boom in railroad required steel which stimulated the mining industry and the coal industry and the telegraph industry and the everyday items to keep the railways and the telegraph and the supply chain operational. The Navy needed ships which stimulated the timber industry and the rope industry and the canvas industry. All of the workers in all of these industries had to be paid and there were not enough greenbacks to pay them, so all the businesses printed their own money to pay their workers. There were also bank-printed notes and then there was money printed by the state governments. There was also currency printed by cities, but that was not enough."

"Where is this history lecture going," Noonan asked.

"I'm getting to the Alaskan part."

"I'm still listening."

"Because there were so few United States government dollars, particularly in the West and the territories, companies also had to pay their employees in their own printed money. This money was called scrip, flickers, clackers, tokens, tickets a lot of other terms, many of them derogatory. If you worked in a mine in Alaska, you were paid in scrip which was good – once again – in the vicinity of the mining company. In another city, not so much.

In the smaller communities, the scrip was actually a blessing. This was particularly true in Alaska when it was both a District and Territory.

Why? Because a trapper, for instance, was only paid once a season. And in one payment, so to speak. So, the trapper bringing his fur to Fairbanks, for instance, would get paid in Fairbanks Bank scrip. The trapper then put the Fairbanks Bank scrip in the Fairbanks Bank – to keep this simple – and when purchases had to be made in Fairbanks, they were 'on the books.' The general store kept a ledger, and the 'money' was transferred from the Fairbanks bank's ledger to the general store's account. There was no exchange of actual things called cash or scrip. This system worked well as long as the purchases were large. But when a child wanted a piece of candy, it was not worth the time of the general store to open its books to deduct a penny's worth of candy from some account. So, the smaller denominations of scrip were a blessing."

"This is going somewhere?"

"Absolutely! And it is part of the missing artifacts from the National Bank of Anchorage Museum collection. The problem in Alaska was the same as it was in the Lower 48. Scrip was only good near where it was printed. If a worker moved, the worker could not take scrip because once out of the area, it was worthless. Think back to the days of the cowboys herding cattle to Kansas City. Once the cowboys got to Kansas City they were paid in local scrip. That scrip was only good in Kansas City. So, the cowboys had to spend every cent they earned in Kansas City because, when they left town, the Kansas City scrip had no value. There was only one way to 'save money,'" Flint made quote marks in the air, "which was to convert some scrip to gold or gold coin. Again, walking around with gold or gold coins was hazardous to your health. Then, after the Civil War, everyone went back to locally printed money and scrip because there was no Plan B.

"In the South there were Confederate dollars. The Confederacy did not have an industrial base. It had a cotton base. Economically this was very good and very bad at the same time. It was very good because the world needed cotton. Specifically, the British. They had an empire that stretched around the world and in every part of the United Kingdom, the important people were expected to be dressed like they lived in London.

"So, they did.

"And that clothing came from England.

82

"Specifically, Leeds.

"Which was buying every bale of Southern cotton it could get.

"This was an economic blessing that kept the South afloat – until it transformed into an unmitigated disaster. The economic blessing came expectedly. The South was selling its cotton to the British and buying all of its war materiel and domestic items from the British. Since there was only one buyer and one seller, so to speak, it did not make sense for 'money' from the cotton bales to be transported from Leeds to Charleston where a plantation owner would spend the 'money' on goods coming into Charleston from England and then the 'money' would be shipped back to England. So, the South developed a financial mechanism that was, again, a blessing at first and then a curse. 'Money' from cotton sales was put in British banks and 'spent' on incoming materiel and domestic product. That way no 'money' had to be exchanged. The sale of cotton was guaranteed by the Confederacy with Cotton Bonds to the planters. When the planters wanted to buy something, they used Confederate dollars that were backed up by the 'money' in the British banks. But again, as in the North, the Confederate dollars were only good in the South. This is the reason the British gunrunners and cotton export sailing crews spent every Confederate Dollar they had because Confederate Dollars were no good outside the South.

"And the system worked.

"Until January 1, 1863. Sadly, courtesy of the deplorable state of American education, the Emancipation Proclamation is the most poorly understood, greatest document in American history. Most people think it freed the slaves. In fact, it did not free a single slave. But what it did do was pull England out of the Civil War. The British had brown and black and yellow people in its colonies and the last thing it wanted was for those brown and black and yellow people to think that because England was supporting the slave states, the British might be thinking about enslaving the brown and black and yellow people in their colonies. The British did not want to start brushfire wars across its empire, so it abandoned the Confederates states.

"What this meant for the South was its paper money became worthless overnight. It had depended upon England to buy Southern cotton and upon England for implements of war. Suddenly England was not buying cotton and selling implements of war. The American Civil War was, in essence, over. Overnight the South went broke. Suddenly, a $100 Confederate Note was worth, well, the paper it was printed on."

Noonan kind of nodded. "Where is this going?"

"It is going to 1933. In that year the United States came off the gold standard. Before 1933, the United States Treasury could only print as many dollars as it had gold to back the printed money. After 1933, the American dollar was not backed up with gold. It was backed up with faith. And to keep that faith, it made the owning of gold illegal. Within months all the bank printed money was gone, and everyone was using American dollars."

"Let me guess," Noonan said. "That didn't include Alaska."

"You got it. Alaska was a Territory and Alaskans were not required to use American money. Not until statehood. But the point of my story, thank you very much for listening, is that between 1933 and 1959, Alaskans kept using scrip. And, since scrip was *not money*, as in American money, a lot of Alaskans dodged the IRS. The reason I am telling you this story is that there were a lot of scrip, bingles, whatever you want to call them in the National Bank of Anchorage Museum. How many I do not know. But what I do know because I am in the business, is bingles do not need a provenance to be sold. Do you know what a provenance is?"

"A document of the history of the artifact. Who bought it originally, for who much, who it was sold to, the whole nine yards."

"Correct. The reason I am telling you is because the bingles from the National Bank of Anchorage Museum were coming to my museum. Now they are not. And no one knows where they went. Cleverly done, someone could flood the market. It's not big bucks, but it's enough to put a small coin dealer like me out of business. I was so concerned I was there when the bingles, the scrip, were packaged. For me. No other museum wanted them. Fine with me."

"Why didn't you take the bingles while you were there? I mean, if you were going to get them anyway, why not just take them then?"

"Johnathan Hemmingway would not let me. He was following the guidelines of the contract Chugach Shipping had with the Aboriginal Artifact Commission. So, he and the two Natives doing the work put the bingles in a crate for shipping. Now the bingles are missing. And, frankly, I'm concerned. I'm a little fish in an ocean of coins but I still need to make a living."

"How much money are we talking about?"

"Depends on the coin. Rare bingles are worth $300 on the market. More numerous coins go for as low as $5. There is no average to work with. From what I have heard, there is a rumor that none of the artifacts can be sold because they do not have a provenance. That's true of artifacts that are one of a kind. Bingles and scrip are not 'one of a kind,'" again he made quote marks in the air. "They do not require a provenance for sale. You probably could not sell the entire collection in Alaska, but in the Lower 48 you could leach the bingles out one at a time and not flood the market."

"What kind of money do you think we are talking about?"

"Cleverly done, about $20,000. But it would take a while. But then again, those sales would be cash so there would be income tax due."

"And no paper trail to follow," Noonan said dryly.

CHAPTER 19

Harrison Anderson at the Aboriginal Artifact Commission was non-plussed. "Jeron Flint has always been a bit off. Nothing illegal, mind you. Just seeing ghosts where they are none." He indicated Noonan should sit in the empty chair beside his desk. But before Noonan could sit, Anderson had to remove a blanket. He indicated the blanket as he tenderly placed on a museum cart on the other side of his desk. "Land of Plenty" robe, Tlingit. I was examining the beaded cross flap to make the sure the buttons were original."

"Have to save the originals," Noonan said with a grin. "They aren't making them anymore."

Anderson smiled. "Not the original ones. We," he indicated the Artifact Commission with a swirl of his fingers, "have to make sure what we are told is original is, in fact, an original."

"Thanks for seeing me on such short notice," Noonan pulled out a sheet of paper. "These are the prices of bingles, Alaskan scrip. Do any of this match what the Anchorage National Bank Museum owned?"

Anderson took the sheet from Noonan and gave it a glance. "Captain, and I did check with the Sandersonville Police Department, and you are legitimate law enforcement, so I have to give you law and order answers. When you here with Bernice Whitcomb you were merely an associate of an insurance company. But now that I know you are law and order, I have to make sure I do not misstate anything.

"Now, let's start with the bingles," he said as he indicated the sheets Noonan had handed him. "First, no one knows if any of the bingles in the National Bank of Anchorage Museum are missing. There has been no theft of artifacts so, at this time, there is no crime. Second, if someone were to steal the bingles from the museum collection, they would have a hard time selling them. Sure, they could offer them on eBay but the only people doing the buying would be Alaskans. There is no market to flood. In about one nanosecond everyone in the bingle collection business would know where the bingles came from. Third, the money is bingles and is in the museum collection, not on sale. Coins become more valuable with age. So, to steal the coins and keep them, everyone is going to know they are stolen even if they do not appear on the market. The artifacts are going to be found and then there will be a reckoning if the bingles are missing. So, in a nutshell, Jeron Flint is baying at the moon."

Noonan nodded. "I understand, but the artifacts are still missing. That's suspicious, you know, in the law-and-order world."

"Captain, Alaska is not Kansas. Things get lost up here all the time. They eventually turn up. Now, since we are talking law and order, keep in mind that the National Bank of Anchorage Museum is not the Louvre, Uffizi, or Tower of London. It did not have valuable items It had artifacts which, by definition, only have historical value. The wealth of a museum is not cash. It is a donation to the museum. It's simply an IRS game. Donations in dollars certainly have a dollar value, but donation of artifacts are a guessing game. The donator puts down the estimated value of the artifact and that's what the IRS accepts as its value. The donor can inflate the write-off by including the cost it took to find the artifact. But that has nothing to do with the artifact. The donor might say the value of the artifact included, say, $1,200 of air flight to the digging, $600 in food and lodging, and $200 in equipment and take that as a write-off against income. But that does not inflate the value of the artifact by $2,000."

Noonan smiled, "Oh, I understand that. Except that the artifacts are missing. Maybe not stolen but missing. The donors, the ones who gave the artifacts, are not out a dime. You, that is, the Aboriginal Artifact Commission, are not out a dime and the museums which were to receive the artifacts are not out a dime. What I do not understand is who benefits from the artifacts being missing. Or stolen."

Anderson grimaced. "Good question. But it's a police question. I can't give you a solid answer, just a guess. And not a very good one at that. The artifacts, all of them, were owned by the National Bank of Anchorage Museum. It collapsed and a nonprofit was formed to see if it could keep the museum open. It couldn't. Six months ago, the nonprofit went belly-up. Then the artifacts were donated – and that is the best word I can use because I am not a lawyer – to museums across the state. It was my responsibility to manage the transfer. The artifacts – and again, at that time, I do not know who actually owned the artifacts at that time since the museum and nonprofit were defunct – were parceled out to other museums And, for the record, Jeron Flint's Museum is a nonprofit. There was security as the artifacts were being wrapped and packaged for the different museums It is possible one or two of the packagers could have snagged an artifact or two, which, I find hard to believe because artifacts have no cash value. Including bingles. The artifacts in crates on pallets were transported to the Anchorage Warehouse and Storage Facility where they were lost. That's it. No crime. No bingles stolen to be flooded on the market. No Mona Lisa to a private collector. Again, Captain, Alaska is not Kansas. Or, in this case, New York, San Francisco or Philadelphia. There's no money in artifacts so I don't see a crime having been committed or about to be committed."

Noonan nodded his head. "I hear you. One last question, what can you tell me about Jerome Hemmingway?"

"Not much. Was a lawyer in Alaska for decades. He wasn't high profile, like defending murderers or pedophiles. Boring stuff. Wills, trusts, bankruptcy, estates, some patents, employment, and some Native rights work. All of it was low profile. Nothing glamourous."

"Do you know when he got Alzheimer's?"

"I've heard that. I met him a few times in Fairbanks in the old days and when he set up the paperwork for the Aboriginal Artifact Commission." Anderson indicated the Commission with a wave of his index finger in the air. "I met him again when he set up the nonprofit to save the museum in the bank. But he was slipping then. We sat around a table and signed documents. Regina and Johnathan told him where to sign and he did."

"If he was that bad off, why was he part of the nonprofit?"

"Good question with a bureaucratic answer. Nonprofits in Alaska must have four members on the Board of Directors. I was one, Regina and Johnathan were two others and then there was Jerome. Four."

"Is the nonprofit still in business?"

"I guess it is on paper. I mean, nonprofits that do not file for renewal with the State of Alaska are considered expired. We haven't met in a while, so I have to assume it's dead. The artifacts are gone so that kind of finishes the work of the nonprofit."

"So, there was no document that ended the nonprofit?"

"Not as far as I know. But there are no artifacts, so there is no reason for the nonprofit to exist. I suspect that sometime next calendar year, the State of Alaska will assume the nonprofit is defunct and administratively bury it."

"Let's hear it for bureaucrats."

CHAPTER 20

Y ou're that 'Bearded Holmes' guy sniffing around town. For the missing artifacts, right?

"Guilty as charged."

Bonnie Roth was the caricature of a museum curator which, in fact, she was. She was a good six inches taller than Noonan, but he had a good 40 pounds on her. Her hairstyle was as close to bald as you could get and still have follicles. She was dressed in a gown that covered her street clothes and footwear that was between boots and shoes. Her voice was high-pitched, she wore glasses with thick lenses and her fingers were covered with rings. Her office was small and had a desk as deep in paperwork as Noonan's desktop in Sandersonville. She had tables along the walls of her office, all covered with piles of papers. There were three file cabinets and behind her desk and above them was the obligatory photograph of the Governor of Alaska. If you work for the State of Alaska, you are always reminded of who is in charge.

"Bonnie Roth," she extended her hand. "Anything I can do to help the Aboriginal Artifact Commission I will do. So, why are you here?"

Noonan smiled, almost silly, "Good question. The quick answer is I asked Harrison Anderson for someone who would walk me through how an artifact ends up in a museum."

Roth smiled. "That's easy. But it is b-o-r-i-n-g, b-o-r-i-n-g, b-o-r-i-n-g, particularly for a cop who chases bad people all over town in speeding cars."

"I've never been that lucky. Detective work is b-o-r-i-n-g, b-o-r-i-n-g, b-o-r-i-n-g, until you get the case to court."

Roth laughed. "OK, I've got time. Do you want me to walk you through the acquisition process?"

"If that's what it's called, yes."

"OK. Follow me. What do you know about museums?"

"Children under 12 are free on weekends."

"Good start."

Roth led Noonan down a long hallway and into a massive room lined with bookshelves. Most of the shelves had boxes but on the bottom tier were bound books. On the back of the bound books were inscriptions like *Ophir Weekly News*, Commissioner Records 1916 -1919, and Wilson Scrapbook. Noonan was led to a table with four chairs and, to his surprise, nothing on the surface.

"I would have expected this table to be covered with papers."

"It was. Until last week. We finished the inventory of the letters, photos, and memorabilia and now they are boxed," she pointed to an upper-tier shelf, "and ready for the public." She indicated one of the empty chairs. "Now, I'm going to start at the beginning. If you already know what I'm talking about, let me know."

Noonan nodded as he sat down and pulled out a notebook.

"Now," Roth said as she pointed around the room, "generally speaking, there are four categories of *properties* – we call them *properties* – in a museum. We happen to have all four here because Alaska is a small state in terms of properties. In a place like Los Angeles or New York, there would be special archives for the properties. Again, generally speaking, the four properties are film and radio recordings, photographs, paper documents and artifacts. The big problem for museums is not storage; it's keeping track of who owns what. And it gets very complicated very quickly. Let's take photographs first."

"Photographs," Noonan asked, "as the individual shots or photographs used in documentaries or photographs bought at an antique store?"

"You are already getting wiser," Roth said and smiled. "Again, generally speaking, a photograph is the property of the person who took the photo, not who *is in* the photo. If the photographer was paid to take the photo, then the photo belongs to whoever paid for the photo. It gets dicey because a photograph of Marilyn Monroe, for instance, could belong to the photographer if he took it on his own. Or the estate of Marilyn Monroe if Marilyn owned the photo when she died. Or whatever movie studio paid for the photograph. But keeping this simple, let's take a photograph taken during the Alaska Gold Rush. Again, it gets complicated, and nothing is set in stone.

"If the photograph was taken before 1922, it is in the public domain. Which means anyone can use it for any reason. B-u-t, if the photographer is known, that photographer owns the rights to the photograph for his lifetime plus 70 years or 95 years after the photo was taken. Maybe. It is nearly impossible for an heir to state that Photograph A-5678 was taken by their grandfather and thus part of his estate. Very few people keep track of personal photographs. Maybe who's in the photographs but not the date the photo was taken."

"So," Noonan said as he wrote in his notebook, "anyone can use a photograph of the Alaska Gold Rush and be pretty sure it was in the public domain."

"Pretty much so. There's also the fair use doctrine. It's a federal statute. You can use photographs that are under copyright in news articles, schools, scholarship, or research. The reason I am starting with photographs is to let you know just how complicated who owns what can be."

"I'm already appropriately confused."

"Good, you'll make an excellent curator."

They both laughed.

"Now," Roth went on. "Moving images and radio recordings are owned by the people who made the films or recordings. When those items are donated to us, the television station or radio station sign the rights over to us. This does not mean the photographs, interviews, or historical footage used are owned by the television or radio station. We just have to take the word of the stations they have followed the correct procedures."

"Do they?"

"In most cases, yes. But it gets hard. If a television station uses footage of a potlatch in Cordova in the 1930s, no one knows who owns that footage. It was probably sitting in someone's attic for three decades before it was donated to a person who gave it to a friend who left it in his will to a museum. It's dicey. For instance, back to Marilyn Monroe, if Marilyn Monroe came to Alaska and was filmed here, the Monroe estate could claim it had to be paid for the use of Monroe's image. Or a movie studio could claim it had paid for Monroe to come to Alaska, so the image is theirs. It gets very complicated very quickly."

"Let me guess, paper documents are the same."

"Yup. Who owns them is very complicated because they were not sold. By that, I mean they have no provenance. Do you know what a provenance is?"

Noonan smiled. "One thing in the museum business I do know. It's a documented list of who owned something, when it was bought, and how much was paid. Kind of a track record of a painting, let's say."

"Correct. Documents do not have provenances. When we get someone's papers, we just have a member of the family sign the rights over to us. Now, and this is important, with the exception of artifacts, which I will talk about next, everything I have talked about so far is in the public domain. In other words, when we get a film clip or a document, it belongs to the public. Members of the public may be barred from seeing them for a number of years, but all the items given to us are State of Alaska property. So, the public can use any information any way it wants, good or bad. We, the museum, do not own the items. The American public does."

"But not artifacts."

"Correct. Artifacts are one of a kind and stay in the museum. Yes, they belong to the public, but are only here on display. Or in the research room. Or here in the archives. The only exception I can think of is a unique Native artifact that some village can prove it owned and was stolen. If that is the case, it will be returned to them. This happens occasionally but not with us."

"How does a Native village prove the artifact was stolen?"

Roth shook her head sadly. "Basically, with historical records. An explorer might write in his journal that he came upon an abandoned village in such-and-such a location and took such-and-such an object. Later it might be discovered that the such-and-such object was donated by the explorer's grandchild to such-and-such a museum, and it is still there. It happens occasionally but for larger objects."

Noonan looked up for his notes. "But not for small items like ivory carvings, blankets, baskets or trade beads?"

"In most cases, yes. They are not unique enough to be specifically identified. The only exception would be if the explorer's descendants donated the objects to a museum. But even then, the explorer could have gone to many villages so it would be hard to specifically state if *this* string of beads came from *that* village."

Noonan shook his head sadly. "Let me guess, those beads do not have a high street value so even if the beads could be identified, it would cost more to get them than if they could be sold for."

"Good observation. This brings me to why you are probably here. Artifacts have no real street value. Sure, you can sell them on eBay, but eBay gets 25% of the sale so we are not talking about a lot of money."

"Then why steal artifacts?"

"There is no reason. As I am sure you have been told, there is no big money in museums. That is, unless there is something of high value, like the Mona Lisa, there is no reason to rob a museum. Like a bookstore. If you are looking to steal for the money involved, why break into a bookstore? The intrinsic value of an artifact or a book is the knowledge you get."

"But museums get money."

"Sure. But not that much. This museum," Roth rotated her finger in the air, "is state funded. We get donations but they are small. Private museums are still nonprofit in the sense they are not businesses. The National Bank of Anchorage Museum was nonprofit when it was established by William Chambers, what, 30 years ago. I'm sure Chambers did it for the love of history and he didn't need any money. But, and again I'm guessing, the instant he established the museum, someone in his family pushed him to make it nonprofit. That gave them a tax deduction when they gave him money."

"The rich getting richer," Noonan sighed.

"Welcome to the history of mankind," Roth said with a sarcastic grin. "But that's the way museum funding works. It's also what keeps the museum alive. Particularly the smaller ones that are not funded by a city, county, state, or the feds. It's a reality of life in the industry."

"OK, so much for funding. Now, walk me through what happens when someone donates an artifact."

"Simple, actually. It comes in the front door, so to speak, and we have the donor fill out a form on which they swear they own the object and are donating it to us. There is a space for them to put any conditions on the donation."

"Like what?"

"Oh, like, we cannot sell the object. If we no longer want or need the object, it goes back to them. Or, if we cannot find another museum to take the object under the same conditions, it returns to them. Rarely do we get anything like that. That's mostly for paper artifacts, like a diary. The family may want the diary of an argonaut who spent his time in Alaska to be in an Alaskan archive, not shipped to Philadelphia."

"How often has that happened?"

"Maybe two or three times in a decade. Most of the time the object is not actually shipped. What happens is a scholar in Philadelphia wants a copy, so we scan it. Then we keep the original and send the scan. It's done in the industry all the time."

"Getting back to the artifacts, once someone signs off ownership, what happens to the object."

"Depends on the quality. If it is better than the artifact we have on display, we switch them. It takes a while because we must rewrite the label. If it is not any better, we store it here. This storage area is about three times the size of the museum. That is, what you call the museum, the galleries and antechambers with artwork and artifacts." .

"How long are the artifacts kept in storage? I mean, the ones you don't use."

"Forever, I guess you'd say. Every once in a while a museum will do a cleaning and toss old artifacts out. But rarely. If there is a cleaning out, like the National Bank of Anchorage Museum, the artifacts are sent to other museums."

"Did all the artifacts from the National Bank of Anchorage Museum get parceled out?"

"As far as I know, yes. Everyone put in a request for items and then they were parceled out. The artifacts from the National Bank of Anchorage Museum are still missing as far as I know."

"No one knows where they are?"

"Nope. Not stolen, that's for sure. There's no money in artifacts. They'll show up. Things in Alaska get lost but sooner or later, they show up."

CHAPTER 21

Johnathan Hemmingway had no problem speaking with Noonan. "I figure you'd get around to me sooner or later," he said over his cup of coffee at the Anchorage Public Library lobby. "All I can tell is what you already know. I delivered the boxes and crates of artifacts from the National Bank of Anchorage Museum in batches to our garage at Chugach Shipping. When all of the artifact crates were gathered, we placed them on six pallets and transported the pallets to the Anchorage Warehouse and Storage Facility. They signed for the crates, offloaded them and I was gone. EOS, End of Story."

"Oh, I know that," Noonan said with a smile. "I wanted to talk to you about the missing staircase."

"Missing what?"

"Staircase. The portion of the staircase at the Anchorage Memorial Hospital. The missing stairs."

Hemmingway looked confused. "What missing stairs?"

Noonan was nonplussed. He feigned a look at his notebook. "I don't have a date, but it was during the remodel of the Anchorage Municipal Hospital. Seems part of the staircase disappeared. A new section had to be ordered and you brought it in."

"Might have. We do a lot of work for the Municipal Hospital. Work," he quickly added, "as in building material we drive in. We had to hire a few more drivers. It's been good for us. Still is. That upgrade is going to take a while."

"But you don't remember bringing in new stairs?"

"Captain, …"

"Heinz."

"Eh?"

"Until there's a crime, I'm Heinz."

"OK, Heinz, what was the question?"

"Do you remember bringing in the stairs?"

"No, not really. Heinz, Chugach Shipping is a teamster company. Since you are not in the industry, I am sure you are unaware of how we operate. All we at Chugach Shipping do is move material. We do not own the material in our trucks. A lot of the material for the upgrade is coming into the Port of Anchorage as cargo. It gets offloaded by stevedores who are the people working on the ships. Once ashore the material is moved by longshoremen and loaded into trucks. We, the teamsters, take the material to its destination. All we do is drive trucks. Sometimes that destination is the Anchorage Warehouse and Storage Facility. Other times it is to business or residence in town. Anchorage is different than other port cities. In a larger city, everything coming ashore would go to a warehouse and be parceled out from there. We're small potatoes in Anchorage."

"The stairs," Noonan prodded Hemmingway.

"I know," Hemmingway replied. "What I am telling you is that we, the teamsters, do the deliveries. We do not own the load we carry. Unless it is visually obvious, we do not even know what we are carrying. And in most cases, we do not even see the load put in our trucks or, for that matter, taken out. For the hospital upgrade, six drivers and I are pretty busy delivering whatevers to the hospital. So, in answer to your question, no, I do not remember any specific load going to the hospital."

"How about loads leaving the hospital?"

"Sure, we do that. Those loads go directly to the landfill on 15th Avenue. It's trash. I'm sure there are some recycles but I can't recall any trips to the recycling center. I think I've been there, what, three times in two years."

Noonan smiled. "I understand. Now, when you get the cargo from the longshoremen, it's in containers, correct?"

"Usually. I mean, the drivers pull up and whatever it is to be moved is in a pile. There might be four or five trucking company drivers there. The longshoremen have the destinations in different piles. Our drivers get handed a sheet of paper which tells them where to take the cargo."

"Who actually puts the cargo into your truck?"

"Longshoremen."

"With forklifts?"

"Usually. Cargo is usually on pallets."

"But a forklift can only put the pallets at the back of the truck trailer. How do you get the pallets all the way to the back of the truck container?"

"Dollys. There are men called dolly hands who move it back. The truck drivers, teamsters, are not involved in the packing of the truck trailers."

"Is that the way the truck trailers are unpacked?"

"Pretty much, yeah. The dolly hands pull the material out of the back of the truck trailer. Unless we are delivering to a private residence or a small business, there are dolly hands-on site who do the offloading."

"Like at the Anchorage Warehouse and Storage Facility?"

"Yeah. Teamsters, we are teamsters, drivers are teamsters, just drive. We do not load or unload."

"What about those loads to the Anchorage Landfill? Do you take dolly hands with you?"

"Usually. Same routine as cargo coming in by ship. But in reverse. We, the teamsters arrive, and the truck trailers are loaded. When we take waste to the Anchorage Landfill, the trucks are already loaded and when we get to the landfill, someone unloads the truck."

"Are there forklifts at the landfill?"

"Usually. Depends on where you are doing the offloading. If you are dumping material from a car or pickup, no. That's at the Central Facility. You just pull up to the edge of a wall of a large warehouse-like building. You toss the items down onto the building floor. Occasionally a bulldozer plows everything into a pile in the back where it gets loaded into dump trucks, and they take it to the landfill lot."

"How often did you or, your drivers, go to the landfill?"

"Why? What does this have to do with the missing artifacts?"

Noonan shook his head in confusion, "I have no idea. All I know is the artifacts are missing. What I have to do, for due diligence, is dot every 'i' and cross every 't.' It's the cop in me. It's just a loose end."

"Fine with me. I don't know anything about any missing stairs. We, the drivers and me, or I, I'm not sure which is grammatically correct, do a lot of business with the Municipal Hospital. We don't want to do anything that will upset that apple cart. I'll tell you what I'll do. I'll get the list of times we went to the landfill. I don't know what good it will do but if that's what you want, fine with me. Anything else you need?"

"Just one more thing ..."

"Detective Columbo is coming out in you, Cap.., Heinz."

Noonan chuckled. "Good one, Johnathan. Just one more thing. I talked with your uncle, I think he's your uncle, the other day. Nice guy. I'm sending him a subscription to *Alaska Magazine*. I didn't see any Alaska reading in his room. Was he better, I mean, coherent when you and Regina established the nonprofit to save the National Bank of Anchorage Museum?"

"Well, first, thanks for the subscription. That was mentioned when I went over to the Senior Home. I don't know if he has the ability to read and understand the articles. He's not doing well. But I'm sure you picked that up. As to your question, sort of. He has been failing for a number of years. When his wife died, ten years ago, he started down the path to Alzheimer's. I don't know if there was a connection, but he went fast. We had to explain the same thing to him multiple times to get his signature on the nonprofit Board. That was the last time he had anything to do with the nonprofit. I see him weekly and let me tell you, it pains me. What he was and what he is. He looks at me and asks who I am. It hurts."

CHAPTER 22

"You want what? Seriously?"

Noonan could hear the disbelief oozing over the telephone line. In this phone, it was a hard line. From his hotel room.

Noonan chuckled. "You're the woman for the job, Bernice. I'm just an interested party in this matter. You, on the other hand, with an insurance company, have some juice, so coming from you, well, people will have a hard time saying 'no.'"

Whitcomb chuckled. "OK, but we've got to talk. Once I start asking for this kind of information, everyone's going to know we are on the trail for something. I mean, Heinz, we are on the trail for something, right?"

"Far as I know, yes. The artifacts are still missing. My bet, the missing artifacts are a red herring. For some reason – and I do not have a clue what that reason is – people want us spinning our wheels looking for the artifacts. I don't want to disappoint them. So, we have to dig around in the dirt to find the real crime. What I'm asking for is just one loose end that might lead somewhere."

"I hate to ask," there was humor in her voice, "are there other loose ends I am going to have to look into?"

"Sorry, yes. Once again, tidbits need to be rounded up. Are they important? I don't know. Right now, I'll still working on those tidbits. But, for the moment, as quietly as you can, see if there are any surveillance cameras at the landfill. Just nose around. Johnathan Hemmingway is going to give me a list of the visits of Chugach Shipping to the landfill."

"What are you looking for?"

"I hate to say it this way, but I do not know. The only solid lead I have, we have, is the disappearance of the stairs. My bet, the stairs were taken at night. The people who removed the stairs most likely came at night when only a watchman was there. The excuse was a late delivery and the night watchman let them in and then went back upstairs on his rounds. Then the men brought something in, the delivery the night watchmen probably signed for, and they took the stairs out."

"But they couldn't take the stairs to the landfill at night."

"Yup. So, we are looking for a delivery to the landfill early the next morning. If they took the stairs, they needed to get rid of them early. Early enough to get back to Chugach Shipping for more loads."

"How about surveillance cameras at the hospital?"

Noonan chuckled. "These folks are thorough. My bet, something went wrong with the system that night. These people are good, Bernice. Why, I do not know yet, but they are good. Very good. And they are moving quickly."

"Do you know why?"

"Not a clue."

CHAPTER 23

"How'd you know that?" Sylvester Flynn looked at Noonan and Whitcomb in disbelief. "How could you possible know we had a security camera failure." He glanced around quickly fully expecting his boss to be within hearing distance.

"We're psychic," Whitcomb said with a sly smile. "No harm, no foul. We're not about to tell anyone. You know, if we ever mention it, that is, if it ever appears in my paperwork, it will be buried deep, deep, deep in some file cabinet in my office. It'll never see the light of day."

"I don't know," Flynn was still jittery. "It's just ..."

"Just nothing, Flynn." Noonan smiled. "We're just an interested party."

"Nah," he said looking at Noonan. "You're a cop!"

"Not in Anchorage. I live about as far away from Anchorage as you can get and still speak English."

"Very f-u-n-n-y," Flynn was not impressed.

"Sylvester," Whitcomb cut in. "I'm in charge here. I'm not a cop. I don't work for the hospital. Once this insurance matter is wrapped up, it's all over. My report goes to no one. It just goes into a file cabinet. Give us the answer and we go away. EOS, End of Story."

"How do I know that?"

"You don't. But it's better for you not to find out. Tell us what we need to know, and we'll be out of your hair. Or, in your case," Whitcomb pointed to Flynn's bald head, "out from under your baseball cap."

Flynn chuckled at that one.

"OK, here's what I know and you," he pointed at Noonan, "close your notebook and put your pen away. I'm only officially talking with her," he pointed at Whitcomb.

"Works for me," Noonan said and held up his arms as if he were surrendering. "I'm just an innocent bystander."

Flynn gave him a give-me-a-break look. "OK, unofficially, and in response to your," he pointed an index finger at Whitcomb, "inquiry, it has come to my attention there has been a glitch in the electronics of the surveillance cameras. Now, keep in mind the surveillance camera in question is old. It was installed about the time Noah loaded the Ark, so breakdowns are not unusual. The glitch lasted about an hour and then recovered, so to speak."

"And there was a delivery during that time?" Whitcomb asked.

"Yeah. I signed for a late-night delivery before the glitch. Then I went on patrol, so to speak. I opened the door for a delivery," he looked at his paperwork, "for Chugach Shipping. I let the truckers in and left. When I returned two hours later, the truckers were gone."

"So, you weren't here when the delivery was made?" Noonan asked.

Flynn looked at Noonan with a blank stare. Whitcomb took the hint. "So, you weren't here when the delivery was made?"

"No. I just signed them in. Late-night deliveries are not unusual."

"But," Whitcomb added, "this was the first time a late-night delivery was not recorded on the security system."

"I don't know that. What I do know is I checked the system when you asked about a specific delivery. That time frame is missing or corrupted or whatever. I cannot say if there were other times when there was nothing recorded."

"When is the security system expected to be upgraded?" Noonan asked.

Flynn came him the same blank stare and then said, "Let's quit playing games here. At night, I'm the only one who comes to this part of the hospital. I am usually on the upper floors, and the bulk of my time is on the main floor of the eastern entrance." He pointed up from the west entrance. "Up there is where I am assigned. When a late-night delivery has to be made, I am called to come downstairs. I open the door and go back upstairs. All I do is open the west entrance door. I do not unlock it. When it closes, it locks automatically.

"As you know, the double doors are not wide enough to admit a truck, so dollies are used. In all cases, including this one," he pointed to Whitcomb's clipboard, "the delivery people exit, the double doors close and lock automatically behind them. Same as the time you are asking about. When I went to check on the delivery, what, three hours later, the truck was gone, and the double door was closed and locked."

"And the security camera recorded nothing."

"Yes. It could have been turned off or the camera unplugged. It's an old camera down here. Anything's possible."

CHAPTER 24

"You're back! And with a partner! The *dynamic duo* arrives!"

Bonnie Roth at the archives waved Noonan and Whitcomb into her office. To make room for Whitcomb, Roth put a pile of papers on the floor behind her desk.

"You know Bernice?" Noonan asked as he sat down.

"She was here before. Missing archives and all. And we know each other from service organizations around town. How's it going, Bernice?"

"Same old, same old. Homeless are still homeless and the Special Olympics is always looking for sponsors."

Roth sadly shook her head. "Ain' that the truth." Then, to Noonan, she asked, "OK, what hocus pocus can I do for you?"

"Just some more questions, loose ends, so to speak," Noonan said as he opened his notebook. "Do you have time for us?"

"All day."

Noonan smiled. "A bunch of unrelated questions. First, is there any chance there was something special in the archives of the National Bank of Anchorage Museum?"

Roth laughed. "Captain, ..."

"Heinz. Until there's a crime, I'm Heinz."

"No crime here," Roth chuckled. "Easy answer. There was nothing special in the National Bank of Anchorage Museum. Even if there were, everyone would know about it when the artifacts were inventoried and divided up. Even if there were something unique, the dollar value would be very low. All the sleazy collectors know where the valuable artifacts are. There were none in the National Bank of Anchorage Museum."

Noonan nodded as he wrote in his notebook. "How about the entire museum? Could the entire museum be sold as a unit? Say, to a Japanese or Chinese collector?"

"Oh, sure, you could sell the entire museum but, again, there is no money in it." She eyed Noonan closely. "If it is the money angle you are looking at. Let's take that first. Now, to get the museum, the entire museum, to say, China, you've have to pack it up and get it to the airport. That didn't happen. We know the archives went to the Anchorage Warehouse and Storage Facility. The archives were logged in. Then they would have to be logged out – which could be done but since there is no money in the archives, it would have to be love, not money. Then the archives would be taken to the Ted Stevens International Airport here in town and be inspected by the Airport Security people, whoever they are for international flights. Then there is the flight cost and on the other end, Chinese customs people will examine the load and file their report. Could it be done? Sure. But why? There is nothing of historical or archival importance to the Chinese. Or, for that matter, the Russians, Japanese, Korean or Pakistani."

Noonan kind of nodded as he wrote. "How about a diary or collection that could be turned into a movie?"

Roth laughed out loud. "Nothing personal, Heinz, but you have to be smoking strong weed to believe that. There is an old saying that you can make a lot of money as a writer, but no one can make a living at it. But, since you asked, let's just pretend what you asked is true. Someone discovers a box of letters and diaries, say, of an Alaska Gold Rush argonaut who discovered something special. The man, or woman, who discovered the papers somehow sneaks them out of the Museum and destroys the paperwork on the papers. That person runs to a publisher and gets an advance of $50,000. And that's a generous advance for a first-time writer. The book becomes a best seller. Sells 100,000 copies."

"Isn't that good money for a writer?" Whitcomb asked.

Roth laughed. "You've been smoking that strong weed too. Let's do the math. Keeping it as simple as possible, the book will sell for $20 in a bookstore. The bookstore will get half the money, $10. Then the writer will get 15% of the money left over, $1.50 per book. Less expenses. The writer will only net $1.50 per book if there are no expenses and, believe you me, every publisher will stick the writer for every nickel of expense for the book. That includes what the publisher pays for a guest appearance, travel to the book signings, newspaper ads, whatever. Next time you see some," Roth made quote marks in the air, "'*knowledgeable author*' on MSNBC, CNN or Fox, keep in mind the publisher is paying for that appearance. And that expense comes out of the money to be paid to the author."

"That could get expensive," Whitcomb said with a voice of shock.

"Absolutely," Roth exclaimed. "The only money in books is when you sell millions. That is, the only money for the author is when the book sells millions. The publisher makes the money. So, if 100,000 copies of a book sell, the author will get $150,000. Out of that $150,000 comes the advance and then expenses. 90% of the books published by the large publishers do not make back the advance. Then the author who got the advance owes the publisher the difference. The chance of some hidden manuscript or diary or letter collection being in the National Bank of Anchorage Museum that will make someone money is very slim."

"How about a photograph?" Noonan asked.

"Ha! You're a dreamer too! Everyone knows what photographs were in the museum. A lot of them are already on VILDA, the visual archive of Alaskan photographs. The historical ones. Those photographs are low resolution. If you want a high-resolution photo, it's $20. If there ever was a valuable one, it is l-o-n-g g-o-n-e. And, to head you off at the pass, there was no artifact in the museum that had high street value. The money for a museum, or, in a museum, is at the other end of the food chain. People and businesses give money for the tax write-off. That's the draw of a museum. Giving to a museum makes you look good publicly and gets you to lower your taxable income.

"How about the money angle," Whitcomb asked. "Can you tell me how museum money is spent?

"Sure. It's easy. All of it is spent and usually with people looking over the books. Museums are not money-makers. So, since you asked, let me take you down a rabbit hole. First, a private museum is rare. Even the National Bank of Anchorage Museum was not private. It might have started that way but by the time it went under, it was a nonprofit. The money for nonprofit museums comes from a variety of sources. The biggest ones in Alaska are federal, state and city grants. But you do not just ask for money and get it. You have to apply for it and jump through the hoops. Then the money is audited by those agencies who gave you the money, you have to file returns with the IRS. Private donors get letters from the museum which they present to the IRS as proof of the deduction."

Noonan fiddled with his pen. "Now, when it comes to the National Bank of Anchorage Museum, it folded when William Chambers died. Then a nonprofit was set up to find money to keep the museum open. Why was the nonprofit formed in the first place? I mean, why not keep giving money to the museum the old way?"

"Good question, political answer. Until Chambers died, the museum space had been provided *gratis*. When he died, the bank said the museum had to start paying rent. The new nonprofit was set up to find rent money to rent the space the museum had been getting for free. Then there was the problem of getting grant money. See, you cannot get federal, state or city money for a nonprofit unless you have been in business for at least two years. The new nonprofit was, well, new. That's why it formed with the Aboriginal Artifact Commission. That's why Harrison Anderson was on the nonprofit. Money for the new museum could be given to the nonprofit because it was a tax write-off. Jerome Hemmingway came up with the concept and designed the paperwork. He's been, how can I say it pleasantly, out of it for a while. Alzheimer's can do that to a body."

"And a mind," Noonan said as he glanced at Whitcomb. "What happened to the money that was raised for the museum?"

"Ah! The cop in you is coming out!" Roth smiled as she said it. "I'm not a lawyer but my guess is that the money raised for the museum is the museum's money. It's the museum's property. Just like the artifacts. So, the money, if there is any left, would be divided up in some manner among the museums getting the artifacts. It's not like there is a pot of money somewhere and people are dipping into the till. All the money coming in was recorded and all of the money going out will be recorded. If not, the IRS will be involved and once the IRS shows up, well, no one is going to be pleased."

"Well, where is the money being kept now?"

"I don't know. I'm assuming it's in an account with the Aboriginal Artifact Commission. That was the fiscal umbrella for the museum after the nonprofit went under."

Whitcomb shook her head. "So, there's paperwork to trace all of the artifacts and the money."

"Better be."

"One last question," Noonan said as he thumbed the pages of his notebook. "The Aboriginal Artifact Commission. Is that a state agency?"

"No. It was set up by the regional Native corporations. It's a nonprofit. It is supposed to be the arbitrator of artifacts between the regional corporations, village corporations, Native nonprofits, traditional councils and the villages. It's a political hot potato. Everyone wants something for nothing. I'm surprised the Commission is still in business."

CHAPTER 25

"Still on the hunt, eh?" Harrison Anderson was up to his ears in paperwork when he looked up and found Noonan in his office. Anderson waved the detective to an empty chair next to the overloaded desk. "have a seat and tell me your troubles."

Noonan sat and pulled out his notebook and made a faux effort to find a blank page.

It didn't work.

"Captain, ..."

"Heinz. Until there's a crime, I'm Heinz."

"Fine with me. Heinz. Anchorage is a small town. You're here for the paperwork and money donated to the nonprofit. No secrets in this town."

"As a matter of fact, yes."

"Not a problem," Anderson leaned back in his wooden office chair. "Before I answer your inquiry, I need to give you some background. If I am telling you things you already know, let me apologize in advance."

"I'm all ears."

"Alaska is not Kansas. Keeping this as mercifully short as possible, before 1972, the era of oil, what the Natives owned and were owed was up in the air. Then came the Alaska Native Claims Settlement Act, ANCSA. Under ANCSA, Natives, in the collective, were given $962.5

million and 104.5 million acres of land. But the 'giving,' so to speak, was not directly to individuals. The law required the Natives, in the plural, to set up local entities, villages, to be established. These were called village corporations and they still exist. There were about 200 of them. The village corporations then created 12 Regional Corporations. There was a 13th Regional Corporation which was to get money but not land because it was composed of Natives who were not in Alaska. That is, the individual Natives in the 13th Corporation live outside of Alaska. They could be in the military, married and living in Detroit, going to school in California, or any of a thousand other reasons Alaskan Natives by heritage were not living within the geographic confines of Alaska. It gets complicated because some Alaskan Natives live in Alaska but do not reside in Alaska. Like on the one Indian Reservation in Alaska, Metlakatla. I hope you have a lot of paper in your notebook to write this down."

Noonan smiled when he looked up. "I'm working on it."

Anderson stretched. "After the village corporations were established, they broke themselves into the 12 Regional Corporations within the geography of Alaska. At that point, the United States government, quite literally, wrote 12 checks dividing up the $962.5 million on a per capita basis and gave the checks to the Regional Corporations. What acres went to which Natives is a rat's nest of politics which I will not go into because you are specifically asking about money."

"Thanks."

"Now, regarding the money, the design or belief or understanding of the federal government was the money which went to the Regional Corporations would filter down to the villages. To a certain extent it did. Sort of. But things got very complicated very quickly. As soon as it was clear there was money for Natives, there was – and still is – a rush for a piece of the pie. Not only did the village corporations want money, so did the village governments. Then many villages formed what are called traditional councils who expected money from the Regional Corporations and, since they were Native, federal and state grant money as well. And many villages formed nonprofits who were also expecting money from the Regional Corporation and, again federal and state grants."

"Keep going," Noonan said as he wrote in his notebook.

"The problem then, and now, is there is only so much money to go around. When there is lots of money, everyone can get a piece of the pie. But as money gets tight, there is not a lot to go around. So, rather than share, all of the entities – Regional Corporations, village corporations, traditional councils, civic government and the Native nonprofits – began fighting for the money available. It was – and is – viscous. Rather than work together, the entities fought – and do fight – tooth and nail for every dollar. Worse, they sabotage the other entities' opportunity. So, in a typical Native village, you have the village corporation fighting the traditional council fighting the village nonprofit fighting the representative of the Regional Corporation and all these people are related to each other. Everyone is accusing everyone else of stealing *their* money and, at the same time, sabotaging everyone else's claims."

"And," Noonan said as he paused in his writing and looked at Anderson, "why are you telling me this?"

"Because," sighed Anderson, "the fighting goes on at all levels. This organization," he spread his arms to indicate the Aboriginal Artifact Commission, "is collectively owned by the Regional Corporations and the village corporations and the traditional councils and receives state and federal funding. There is the possibility of a lot of money on the table, and everyone wants a cut of the action. The only saving grace is we deal with artifacts and how they are distributed. You can negotiate how to divide up a federal grant of $600,000 but when it comes to bones or ivory carvings, they have to go somewhere intact."

"Seem logical to me," Noonan muttered.

"Now, to the money in the nonprofit from the National Bank of Anchorage Museum, it is just as complicated. After the death of William Chambers, the National Bank of Anchorage wanted rent money for the space occupied by the museum. Chambers was deceased so, as you know, a nonprofit was established. Jerome Hemmingway, when he was coherent, wrote up the legal paperwork and was a partner. You must have a Board of Directors of four to be a nonprofit in Alaska. Regina and Johnathan Hemmingway were on the Board. I had to be on the Board for three reasons. One, I was the authority on Alaskan artifacts.

Two, I represented the Aboriginal Artifacts Commission. And three, to get federal and state funding, specifically, you have to have been a nonprofit for at least two years. The museum nonprofit had just formed but the Aboriginal Artifact Commission had been in existence for a lot longer. So, any state or federal money for the museum would have come through the Aboriginal Artifact Commission."

"So," Noonan noted in his notebook, "when a check was written for the nonprofit trying to save the museum, it was written to the Aboriginal Artifact Commission."

"Not the way you mean it. If someone, an individual, or a business wrote a check to the nonprofit, the money went directly into the nonprofit's account. If the check came from the feds or the state or even a city government, it went to the Aboriginal Artifact Commission. But that's the simple explanation. Yes, the money went into separate pots, so to speak, but most of that money was specifically earmarked for specific items. Again, keeping this as simple as possible, a village corporation wants ten artifacts from the old National Bank of Anchorage Museum to be sent to the village. So, it applies for money from the Regional Corporation for the artifacts. The Regional Corporation funnels some money that was destined for that village into the acquisition of the artifacts. Then the Regional Corporation adds the dollar to its annual request for funding from the state and federal government and maybe some other grant applications. The money comes in and the village is informed it is going to get the artifacts. Now the fighting begins. Where are the artifacts to be displayed? In the village corporation office? In the traditional council office? In city hall? Every place wants to display the artifacts because the grant money includes display money. And money for a curator. And money for overhead. And money for security. So, who gets that money? Worse, it's not like there are a million dollars on the table. So, the less money there is, not the more fighting there is."

"What happens to the money until the fighting stops?" Noonan asked.

"The simple answer is it sits with the nonprofit administratively."

"But the nonprofit does not exist anymore."

"That is correct. But that doesn't matter. The money brought in by the nonprofit has already been distributed. That is, when the artifacts were divided up, each individual collection, so to speak, had an earmark of money from the nonprofit. The distribution has already been made. The money, as in the spendable cash, is with the Aboriginal Artifact Commission. When a village gets the actual artifacts and decides how the money for display, security, overhead, etc. will be spent, a request will be made to us, and we will send the money."

"So how much money are we talking about," Noonan asked.

"Heinz, as a cop you are used to specific answers. It does not work that way in the museum world. There is the cash from donations which amounts to about $30,000. Then there are commitments that are part of grant applications. Then there are pledged moneys which will only be given when certain conditions are met. Those conditions could be met tomorrow or next week or a year from now. On top of that, there are moneys in bulk which have to be sorted out as to who gets what. AND, on top of *that*, all money matters have to be allocated by the Board of the Aboriginal Artifact Commission. It's not as simple as reaching into an account and pulling money out."

"But," Noonan said, "there is at least $30,000."

Anderson shook his head. "No. $30,000 was *donated*. The moving expenses are taken out of that. And the hiring of the staff to divide the artifacts, both on paper and physically in the old museum was taken out. Those expenses have to be taken out of the $30,000."

"Well, how much is left?"

"Again, it's not that simple. The staff dividing the artifacts was paid as the work was being done. So, the checks came from the Aboriginal Artifact Commission. Transferring the money from the nonprofit account to the Aboriginal Artifact Commission for the work happens at the pleasure of the Board. That's about once a month. If the Board takes up the issue. But the payment for the staff dividing the artifacts is so small and the other financial matters so large, putting off the authorization is routine. Then there is the matter of where the money being paid is coming from. Is it from the nonprofit that no longer exists or from a federal or state grant through the Aboriginal Artifact

Commission or was it part of a specific pledge if the artifacts in question went to a specific village?"

"Well, overall, how much money are we talking about?"

Anderson shook his head. "I have three answers. First, the specific money donated to the nonprofit as cash was $30,000 and how much is left after repaying the Aboriginal Artifact Commission for money spent is unknown. Second, pledged money is in the range of $100,000 but that is not money in hand. It is money that will be paid when certain conditions are met. Then there are state and federal grant moneys which, again, have certain administrative strings attached. That could be about $200,000. But there is not an account with $330,000 and even if there were, the money would only come out piecemeal as approved by the Board of the Aboriginal Artifact Commission."

"$330,000 is a lot of money."

"In your bank account for you, yes. But over a ten-year period for 20 or 30 small museums, not so much."

"Are the financial requests by the museums available for examination?"

"Again, yes and no. Yes, the actual division of the dollars both available and pledged or anticipated was certified and included with the division of the artifacts. No, the paperwork is with the artifacts and as you know, they are currently missing."

And a distant gong reverberated deep in Heinz Noonan's cerebral cortex.

CHAPTER 26

As the old saying goes, the difference between in-laws and outlaws is that in-laws are not wanted. That being said, summers in Alaska are incomparable to anywhere else on earth. The same could also be said about winters. But, in Noonan's case, he only spent a few weeks a year in Alaska and those weeks were in June and July.

But he had to put up with his in-laws.

Again, that being said, in-laws, like Alaskan summers and winters, were incomparable. Some in-laws were a pleasure. Others not so much.

Noonan's week on the prowl ended on Friday morning and then he was off with the relatives for the State Fair. The twins had left for summer school, maybe, or, more likely, at some summer event, or events, which they used as an excuse to leave Alaska earlier than returning to North Carolina with Noonan and his wife. This was fine with the two Noonans because it was two fewer people to ferry about for fishing safaris, borrowing the rental car for an evening or, worse, an afternoon in some Alaskan enclave like a tourist ant hill.

Tourists in Alaska boggle the sane. Noonan found it amazing that anyone with a high school education, much less a college degree, would believe the myths of Alaska. The state does not have six months of 24-hour-a-day sunshine followed instantaneously by six months of unbroken darkness. Grizzly bears did not haunt the city streets during the night and while salmon are plentiful in the streams, you cannot just reach into the water and pull them out by the handful. Yes, there are ice worms but not large enough to put on a fishhook and the only igloos are the namesake shipping containers at the airport.

The State Fair was a perennial joy because there was always something new to see. The Noonans did not attend the North Carolina State Fair because it was too far from Sandersonville for a pleasant afternoon sojourn. But the Alaska State Fair was in Palmer, 30 miles from Anchorage and if you took the train, which the Noonans preferred, you did not have to fight the Alaskan traffic – which had had too many drivers who did not know what the white lines on pavement meant.

Sunday was the inevitable visit to a church, the specific congregation depending upon which church the two Noonans had not visited over the past month of Sundays. The Noonan barbeques were enjoyable because there was usually fresh halibut, a delicacy that was available in Sandersonville but with fish so frozen they took a month of Sundays to defrost and by then the tastiness was gone. The same could be said of salmon in North Carolina.

Monday was July 4th so everyone associated with the missing artifacts was taking the day off with pay. It was not until Tuesday afternoon that Noonan, the detective, was able to break free of his obligation to go shopping with his wife and escape to the office of Bernice Whitcomb.

After Noonan told of his three-day weekend with relatives, Whitcomb laughed. "My family is in Cleveland and my husband's family is in Detroit. We're all alone up here in Alaska, boo-hoo. You know the George Carlin joke of families?"

"Not sure."

"He said, 'The other night I ate at a family restaurant. Every table had an argument going.'"

"Nice, I like the George Burns quote, 'Happiness is having a large, loving, caring, close-knit family in another city.'"

"That's as good as the Carlin quote. Now, humor aside, I have some information for you."

"And I for you," responded Noonan.

"I love it when we can share," Whitcomb smiled. "You first."

"Well," Noonan began. "Keep in mind I think like a cop. When in doubt, look for the money. If it's a murder, look for jealousy, revenge and idiocy. But a lot of the time it's money as well."

"So," Whitcomb asked as she pulled her clipboard off her desk. "Where's the money?"

"Good question. I don't know. I think I knew what was happening but it's just loose pieces of information. I live in three different worlds. There is what I can prove, what I know but cannot prove and what I suspect. I'm in that third world right now."

"Thrill me."

"Through a convoluted system of raising money for the National Bank of Anchorage Museum, the nonprofit pulled in a lot of money." Whitcomb started to whistle but Noonan stopped her mid-whistle, "But it is not as easy as just finding the bank account. Money is in many forms. Some cash and a lot of promises. All the money was washed through the Aboriginal Artifact Commission which could mean the money is still there or it's been leached out. I was involved in grant writing a number of years ago and the $500,000 we got vanished through expenses that did not actually exist."

"Did not exist?"

"Right. Like a certain percentage for management, some money for overhead, profit, and consultants. It was all legal but when it came time for the weeds – I call the actual work in-the-weeds – there was only 10% left. Of the $500,000 received, only $50,000 went to the people actually doing the work. That's the way the system works."

"That's happening here?" Whitcomb shook her head in disbelief.

"Maybe. But right now, nothing illegal has happened. Money has been collected and put in different accounts. Those accounts have oversight which means no money comes out without the approval of the Board of Directors of the Aboriginal Artifact Commission. Yes, there is money there. No, I do not know how much. Yes, there is a chance some will get siphoned for dubious purposes. No, I cannot prove it. All I can do for the moment is wait for the Board of Directors to do something."

Whitcomb laughed. "It has been my experience that boards of directors have a lot better things to do other than make decisions. And, if the

Board of the Aboriginal Archive Commission is dealing with megabucks from the federal government, state government, grants, and sole source contracts, a few hundred thousand is a drop in the bucket."

Noonan nodded his head. "I agree. But, thinking as a cop, at this point there is only one suspicious aspect of the money angle. According to Harrison Anderson, the actual division of some of the money has already been done. That is, an initial determination of some of the money has already been made."

"Really?"

"It's another one of those yes and no answers. Yes, it has been made. No, we cannot see it because the paperwork is with the artifacts and the artifacts are missing."

"I don't see the connection."

"I don't either. As I see it, the money, whatever amount it is, is locked in place until the artifacts are found."

"R-i-g-h-t. Then there is going to be a donnybrook over who gets what money. You don't live up here but let me tell you, when it comes to money and Natives, it is a maze. And by Natives, I mean the Regional Corporations, the village corporations, traditional councils, Native non-profits, Native-owned businesses, and these people are not happy campers when it comes to money. All of them only want one thing: more."

Noonan nodded. "Probably true. But that's not our concern. When the money comes, it will be up to the Board of the Aboriginal Artifact Commission to divide the pie. Our job," Noonan pointed to Whitcomb and then himself, "is to find the artifacts. Now you know everything I know. What do you know that I do not?"

Whitcomb laughed. "I wish I could be as productive as you. I could get the computer readout of the trips Chugach Shipping went to the landfill. There are two sides to the landfill, one for large loads and the other for dumping by hand. There have only been three trips to the large load area of the landfill, and they were months ago. But there have been visits to the hand dumping area. About every three or four days. Most were in the afternoon. Two were in the morning. One of those was at 11:30 which is pretty close to 'afternoon,'" Whitcomb made quote marks in the air. "The other was at 8:15 a.m. Right after the landfill opened.

It opens at 7:30. Only problem: the date is wrong. That is, we know when the stairs disappeared and if Chugach Shipping had burned a path to the landfill to get rid of the stairs, the truck would have shown up the next morning. That's not the case here. The early morning visit was three days later."

"Any idea what was in the truck trailer then?"

"Nope. No weight either. Trucks just show up, pay their fee, and drive into the Central Transfer Station. Then the dumping is done by hand. Or dolly. Chugach Shipping has a monthly pass so when one of its trucks shows up, it is just waved through."

"So, there is no way of knowing what was in the trailer?"

"No. I checked to see there was security footage and I was told no. The camera is not set to record what gets dumped, but to make sure there are no accidents in the drive-up area. There's also a good chance that morning's recording is long gone. I mean, we are talking about, what six weeks ago."

"Tough break."

"Not really. I checked with the teamsters and got a list of drivers. Gypsy drivers, that is. These are drivers who are available for hire. Not gypsy truckers; gypsy drivers."

"Sorry. What's the difference?"

"A gypsy trucker is a teamster who has a truck. He bids on jobs. He doesn't work for anyone or any company all the time. The key here is he owns a truck and when you hire him – or her – he – or she – uses their own truck. A gypsy driver is a teamster who does not have a truck. He – or she – gets hired by the hour, day, or job. He – or she – works as long as the employer wants."

"So how do we trace the gypsy driver?"

"Through payroll. I got more than a dozen names and pared them down to three."

"So, we've got three men to contact?"

"Two. One's a woman. And let me tell you, Heinz, she is a firecracker."

CHAPTER 27

When Bernice Whitcomb had told Noonan Lael Morgan was a fire-cracker, she was not kidding. There were other terms for a woman like Morgan, all of them complimentary but none fit to print. The problem wasn't finding Morgan; it was getting her to stay on subject.

"Socialism, Captain."

"Heinz, until there's a crime, I'm Heinz."

"Fine, Heinz. Let me tell you, I spent three sessions as a legislative aide. I don't know how smart legislators were before they went to Juneau, but with the first step off the plane for a session they lose half the IQ points they have. They are supposed to go to Juneau to solve problems, not make them."

Noonan let Morgan rage. "I agree. It's the same with all legislatures. And, as a matter of fact, with the United States Congress."

"What we need is more socialism, Heinz. Not socialism as in the whole government, but the critical parts. Health care is a hot one. Do you know how many truckers I work with are injured and don't have the money to see a doctor? Did you know the Number One cause of bankruptcy in America is unpaid health care costs? That's crazy. If you're poor, your health care should be paid for. Make money and you have to pay your own health care costs. Hey, in England all health care costs are paid by the state. Well, in that case, the British government. But here in the good old US of A, you're on your own."

"I can see your point. But I want to take a moment of your time to ask about some driving you did for Chugach Shipping."

"Good people. Pay on time. Regina is high quality. Her brother, Johnathan, is a few sandwiches short of a picnic."

"OK, but I'm interested in the work you did for Chugach Shipping. Seems you have done a lot of driving for them."

"Good people. Pay on time. Regina is a fine businesswoman. Johnathan is always asleep at the wheel."

"I see. Now, how many times in the last month did you drive a Chugach Shipping truck to the landfill?"

"Oh, maybe a dozen."

"All to the landfill or some to the Central Facility. You know, where the truck trailer is emptied by hand."

"Both are. In most cases I have someone with me when I go to the landfill. On the other side, the other one, in the Central Facility, I do it myself. Use a dolly but I'm by myself."

"How large are those loads?"

"Not very. If they were large, they'd go to the landfill."

"Well, how large were the loads you took to the Central Facility."

"Do you know how little those men and women in the solid refuse department make? Not enough. City doesn't pay them squat. And their retirement takeout is about 2%! 2%! How are those folks supposed to live when they retire? Probably never will! We've got to pay our workers more. They are the backbone of the economy. Every dime they spend is here in Anchorage. Pay your people more and they spend more. The economy gets better. Start taxing the rich, Heinz. It is Heinz, right? Do you know I pay more in taxes than guys like Steve Jobs and Elon Musk –COMBINED! And their companies skate! Skate! We have, what, 800 homeless people on the city streets and big companies in Anchorage don't pay diddly in taxes. They say they are getting oil for us. BS. We get a fraction of the value of the oil. Then there are the Native corporations! They're just businesses. Same as the oil companies. They have homeless shareholders on the street, drunks, mentally ill Natives who need help and the Native corporations don't do diddly. Say they are 'businesses' and not responsible for the homeless and the drunks and the mentally ill. And the Anchorage Assembly is doing nothing and the mayor is doing nothing and the governor is doing nothing and the Native corporations are raking in huge profits."

"I understand," Noonan was calming. "It's a shame."

"It's more than a shame. It's downright *illegal.* The Alaska Native Lands Claims Settlement extinguished all aboriginal rights. That's a quote from the law. But the Native corporations still get sweetheart deals from the federal government. That's not socialism; that's corruption."

"Possibly true. We can discuss that later. I just need to know what kind of trash you dumped out of your truck when you went to the Central Facility."

"Which time?"

"Oh, how about all of them?"

"I'd say I went a half-dozen times. I'd get in a Chugach Shipping truck and drive to the hospital and wait while the truck trailer is loaded. Then I'd drive to the landfill or the Central Facility. At the landfill, I'd be with someone or someone with a forklift would pull the junk out of the back. At the Central Facility, I'd do the heavy lifting."

"Six times to the Central Facility?"

"About right."

"Ever go there in the morning?"

"Once. Early. I got to Chugach Shipping, and they were loading the trailer. Not a large load, a lot of lumber, some mattresses, drywall and some busted toilets and bathroom sinks. I think they'd been storing a lot of junk for a while and decided it was time to ship it out."

"Was the truck loaded when you got it?"

"I just got there, and the truck was ready to go."

"So, how do you know what was in it?"

"I was the one who dumped the garbage. Had a dolly. Not a lot of material but enough to take about an hour to offload."

"Do you remember the lumber?"

"Not well. Odd 'cause it wasn't shattered or splintered like a lot of other wood I've taken before."

"Anything else odd about the load?"

"Odd because it was in the morning, and the truck was already loaded."

Noonan smiled and then went oblique. "You said Regina was a fine woman. Any particular reason for saying that?"

"She gives me no guff. Do you know what it is like being a woman in this business? This is a man's business. Be a woman and try to get a load for a truck! Bankers expect you to get a man and stay in the kitchen. Regina makes sure I'm a top priority for any job. I love her for that. Her brother, Johnathan, is a worm. If he could he'd sit around in the office all day and play solitaire on the computer. If he weren't related to Regina he'd be on unemployment. She's the brains of that company."

Noonan went oblique. "I'm also impressed with her. She tried to save the National Bank of Anchorage Museum."

"Sure did. Almost made it. Had to go into business with Harrison Anderson. That will be a mistake."

"Really?"

"He's one of those corporate Natives. We call them 'suits' or 'red apple Indians.' Parlay their Nativeness for cash. Could care less about Natives. It's all about the money."

"Oh, so he's crooked?"

"Men like Anderson are not crooked. They're political. Find a scheme and stay on the good side of the law. Stick other people with the disaster. We call it 'coming out of the water dry.' Nothing will ever happen to him, but he will leave a trail of disaster behind him."

"Like Regina?"

"Doubt it. She's skookum. That's Alaskans for 'very smart.' Does not make a move without considering every angle there is. Nay, if Harrison Anderson is planning something Regina is not going to end up on the short end of the stick."

"How about Johnathan?"

"An idiot. He's the kind of person who would invest a fortune in cryptocurrency and then wonder why he's broke."

Then Noonan took a wild punch, "How long have you lived in town?"

"My whole life. Married twice. Saved myself twice. Why?"

"Well, you know about the missing artifacts?"

"Everybody does. They're not stolen. Just lost."

"Ever meet Regina's uncle, Jerome?"

"Sure. Sharp lawyer. Was, anyway. When I knew him. He was the brains behind the formation of the Aboriginal Archive Commission."

CHAPTER 28

As it turned out, it was so easy to find information on the Aboriginal Artifact Commission Noonan kicked himself for not pulling up the information before. It had been formed as a nonprofit Native corporation three years earlier and had a Board of Directors of four. Noonan could find no reference to Jerome Hemmingway as the lawyer for the group, but Regina was a Board member. When he pulled the group up on the directory of foundations and found it was actually a charity, not that Noonan knew the difference. Over the past three years it had taken in a modest amount of money, much of which was spent on staff and office expenses. Harrison Anderson had a salary of $200,000. Board expenses were $100,000, most of it travel and per diem. There were several ongoing contracts, none of them associated with Regina.

The website for the Aboriginal Artifact Commission was sparse and did not list any staff by name. But it did list the four Board members by name. Regina was one. So was Harrison Anderson. The other two were credited as movers-and-shakers from traditional councils in villages Noonan had never heard of. One was Henry Kagoona and the other was Steven Salinas. Kagoona was clearly a Native name, Salinas was not. There was a contact page that did not work. Harrison Anderson was listed as the Executive Director and the contact for him was via the contact page.

A search of the internet for Jerome Hemmingway just pulled him to a web page for his law practice and the email link on that page did not work. On the Alaska Bar Association web page, he was listed as having an expired law license and there had been no investigations of him or his practice. Pulling up the case files for the Alaska courts, Jerome Hemmingway was frequently listed as an attorney of record but not as a plaintiff or defendant. The same was true of Harrison Anderson and Johnathan Hemmingway. Regina had a long list of legal cases, almost all of them as plaintiff for unpaid bills. She had one speeding ticket which was dismissed. On the Federal court case file list, there was no mention of Jerome Hemmingway, Johnathan Hemingway or Harrison Anderson. Regina had one charge, clam poaching, which resulted in a $100 fine.

"Clam poaching?" Noonan muttered to himself. "Why would anyone steal clams?"

An internet search for Johnathan and Jerome pulled up nothing but bios which were, in the case of Jerome, well out of date. There were quite a few pages on Harrison Anderson. White father and Yupik mother. Father had started as a banker in Nome and married a local girl. He was promoted to a bank job in Fairbanks and by that time the family had three children. The oldest, Harrison, had gone off to college in San Francisco on one of the early scholarships for Natives. One of the children, the only daughter, had died in an accident in elementary school. Harrison's brother had graduated from high school and was operating a fly-fishing operation in the Fort Yukon area.

Harrison was the star of the family and the newspapers detailed how he had developed the Aboriginal Artifact Commission because the owner of the National Bank of Anchorage Museum had a "medical problem" and could no longer handle the day-to-day duties of running a museum. This fit with what Noonan had been told. Noonan checked the date of the formation of the nonprofit and found the dates matched. The obituary for William Chambers appeared six months later. There were kudos for his support of the "Alaskan culture, White and Native," and a statement from Harrison Anderson that the "work of the museum would continue' and donations to help the museum survive are being requested.

Then something unexpected happened.

Nothing.

Nothing, as in the internet went blank with no mention of the museum, the nonprofit or the Aboriginal Artifact Commission. There was no reference to any of these in the newspaper archives either.

Zip.

Why?

CHAPTER 29

Hollywood would never have to find someone who looked like a newspaper reporter. All Hollywood would have had to do was film James Hayworth at work. He throbbed newspaper. He was about 5 feet six, five feet in elevation and six feet around. He was dressed as if he slept in his clothes, had not shaved since Bill Clinton was President of the United States, and had a coffee maker on the side of his desk.

Hayworth waved Noonan into his office, actually a cubicle plastered with old newspaper copy. He had a snapshot of a woman in a bikini above his computer and beside it, a photograph of two couples on the beach. Noonan instantly recognized Bernice Whitcomb. Her husband towered over the other three.

"Jerry told me you wanted to talk," Hayworth said as he pointed at the photograph. "And he said I would get the breaking news on the scoop when it comes."

"You are at the top of my list," Noonan said with a smile.

'Have I heard THAT before," Hayworth said and laughed. "Jerry said you were a cop on some kind of a secret assignment. OK, what can I do for John Law?"

"Let me give you some names. Tell me what you know off the record. I've searched the newspaper archives and found nothing."

"Well, there could be a reason for that."

"We'll see," Noonan opened his notebook. "Jerome Hemmingway."

"Ah, the Hemmingways. Old Fairbanks family. Well placed. Were. Father was a white airline pilot servicing the bush. His wife was a Native from Kotzebue. It was their business, the airline. Both were sharp as tacks. Made money in a tough business. He spoke three Native languages which helped big time. Parents died in a plane crash and left two children as orphans, Regina was about 12 and Johnathan, maybe, seven. Jerome, the uncle, took in the two kids. Regina is a kickass bit.., er, individual. Works her butt off. She was and is successful in anything she does because she works hard. Johnathan, well, he's a black hole. Cannot do a thing right. Flunked out of high school. High school! In Alaska! He's about five years younger than Regina. By the time he dropped out, she had started her own company, Chugach Shipping, and she took him on as an employee. Not an owner, an employee."

"How about Jerome," Noonan asked.

"Sharp. Very sharp. V-e-r-y sharp. Must run in the Hemmingway family. One of those behind-the-scenes guys. Doesn't want kudos or news articles. Not a criminal lawyer, if that's what you're asking, but boring stuff like corporate filing, patents, estates, wills, and trusts. He's never talked to me. Whenever I asked him a question, he told me to go talk to the person in charge. But he was the man to go to when you needed the boring paperwork done right the first time."

"Seen him lately?"

"Never saw him that much to begin with."

"I was told he was the brains behind the Aboriginal Artifact Commission."

Suddenly there was a l-o-n-g moment of silence.

Noonan sat for a l-o-n-g time as well and then said, "Let's get real, James. There's something afoot. When someone from out of town can figure it out, you know…"

Before he could finish, Hayworth looked around as if someone might be eavesdropping on his answer. "Listen, Captain,.."

"Heinz. Until there's a crime, I'm Heinz."

"Well, then, we'll stick with 'Captain.' First, because I never want it said I lied to a cop, even one from out of state. Second, there are a lot of rumblings. That's my way of saying I've heard a lot but not a lot of things that make sense."

"Why not tell me what you've heard, and I'll tell you what I can."

"Nope. We're going to reverse that."

"OK. But this will be confidential until something breaks."

Hayworth kind of shrugged. "You have my word but it's not worth much. After all, I'm a reporter."

"OK, I'll be deepthroat."

"Works for me. Whacha got?"

Five minutes later Hayworth got himself a cup of coffee. Noonan declined the offer of a cup of Joe. "I don't drink coffee after 11 a.m."

"I drink it all day, (pause) and into the night when I have to. I had not heard of the missing artifacts but, frankly, that's not much of a story. The collapsing the National Bank of Anchorage Museum is not much of a story either. I had not heard of the missing staircase and, you know, if you were not a cop, I'd have dumped the story. Even all together there isn't much. But what makes my heart beat fast is the connection to the Aboriginal Artifact Commission."

"You think it's crooked?"

"I know it's crooked! I'm just waiting for the facts to rise to the surface of the cesspool."

"Can you tell why you think it's crooked?"

"You'd have to be an Alaskan to understand."

"I'm married to an Alaskan and I've been hearing that excuse for 43 years."

Hayworth laughed. "I've been hearing that from my wife for 27 years. The Commission is one of those ongoing Native scams There is a lot of money for Natives, federal and state, as long as they play the game right. Playing the game right means living up to the requirements of the grant. Then, one day, the Commission disbands. Its records disappear. Any money left vanishes. No one knows anything. It's hard to get people to talk and after chasing people for a few years, the investigation goes away. "

"What makes you think the Commission is a scam?"

"Well, first, there are not enough Native artifacts to have a Commission. Second, there is already a museum association to do the same job. Third, half the Board of Directors is from outside of Anchorage. They rarely meet so all decisions are made by the staff. A staff of one: Harrison Anderson."

"Does he have a record of any kind?"

"I couldn't find one. No arrests for anything. No court cases, here or with the feds. Graduated from Berkley and a law degree from Hastings in San Francisco. Good schools, both of them. Spent time in the Army, two tours in Vietnam, as a military lawyer. Some time in practice in San Francisco, no trouble I could find, and then he came to Alaska. Why? I do not know. My guess, only one I have that makes sense, Jerome Hemmingway. If that's true, something is being cooked up."

"You think Regina could be involved?"

"Tough questions. She's pretty straight. Not really. I see her as a Native who is interested in Native issues and Native artifacts. I also don't see her as someone who will take the money and run. Harrison Anderson, probably. He has no ties here. Regina does. My guess, Regina is clean. A pawn. A patsy. A name to be used locally. But if I were going to point any fingers, I'd say Johnathan. He's not smart enough to know he's being used."

CHAPTER 30

There comes a time in all investigations when the investigator is lost. Crime fighting is not all beer and skittles. Far too often the public believes that investigations are as streamlined as an episode of LAW AND ORDER. Hollywood and the silver screen have trivialized both the investigation of the matter and then the prosecution of the perpetrator. In fact, a lot of criminals 'get away with it.' The cleverest of criminals are never caught. It's not as if they slip through the legal system; it's just that their crime is never reported. Competent jewelry thieves steal precious stones and then sell the gems back to the insurance company that must cover the loss. The burglar will 'sell' the merchandise back for a percentage of its worth. The insurance company is pleased to pay the burglar 15% of the worth of the stolen items rather than 100% of the value of the theft.

It is certainly true that the larger the prize, the greater the chance of being caught. But the flipside to the truism is that it takes a lot of forensics to catch clever thieves. The keyword to escape justice is 'thief.' In cases of murder, rape, pedophilia, kidnapping and other violent acts, there is a victim, and the victim has family and friends. This means unrelenting pressure on the authorities to 'do something.'

Further, alas, the family has usually been mesmerized by cases on DATELINE or FORENSIC FILES where the perpetrator is caught. What the interested parties do not realize is investigations take a lot of time and the most pressing cases come first. A cold case file is called a cold case file for a very good reason; **hot** cases come first.

In terms of what he had; Noonan had zip. What had started out as a modest investigation into why Native bones were delayed in reaching a museum, he had stumbled into a jungle of details with no pathway through or out of the overgrowth. He could not go back, and he could not go forward, and every other direction looked the same.

Worse, unlike both a case on LAW AND ORDER and in real life, there was no 'back to the beginning' to return to in this matter. What he had was a cold case in the making. On top of that, there was not a single item – usually called a clue – which indicated a crime had been committed. In real-world terms, there was every possibility that the artifacts were, indeed, misplaced. Not a single dollar that had been paid to or collected for the museum had been spent or disappeared so there was no theft. Yes, there were strong hints of impropriety but, in a court of law, *impropriety* was not evidence. Again, what he had was zip.

However, the experienced sleuth he was, Noonan knew there was never a time when you abandoned an investigation because there was no 'beginning' to return to. He did have a mountain of facts. What had he missed? Was there anything he had neglected to ask? What tidbit had slipped through the cracks? While he had no 'beginning' to return to, he did have pages of notes and into those he dove.

CHAPTER 31

The problem with tidbits was they were, well, tidbits. Worse, there was often minutia. While a tidbit is a morsel of something pleasant, usually food, minutia has nothing to do with something pleasant, tasty, or worthy of a shred of enthusiasm. Every case has a dump truckload of minutia. The problem is sifting through the chaff. Sometimes there was a kernel of a lead. Other times, not so much.

After two days of examining his notes, between barbeques with in-laws and some summer theater, Noonan found a number of items that bore a closer look. This did not mean the items were worthy of intense investigation or something important he had overlooked. Further, they could not be called 'loose ends' either. They were just minutia that needed a bit more clarity.

His first call was to Lael Morgan. It took a while to track her down. He finally got her on the electronic Beelzebub while she was waiting for a selection of pallets to be loaded into the truck trailer she was going to drive to the landfill.

Her opening remark was predictable. "Want more reasons to pay people more?"

"You've convinced me already. Do you have time for a few more questions?"

"I've got 'til the trailer is loaded."

"Great. When we last talked, I asked about your early morning trip to the Central Facility."

"Yeah."

"If that facility is like the ones in North Carolina, where you back your vehicle against a low cement wall and then dump the contents of your vehicle over the wall. Then it falls a dozen feet onto a cement slab which is occasionally cleared by a bulldozer."

"Yeah."

"Is that way it is Anchorage?"

"Yeah."

"Well, what you said, what I wrote down, was your statement that you used a dolly. That implies that the stuff you were dumping was not in the front of the trailer.

"Yeah."

"Was the stuff you dumped at the back of the trailer, or did you have to move it from deeper in the interior to the back of the trailer to dump it?"

"Humm, you cops ask wild questions. As I remember, it was at the back of the trailer. That is, against the wall that divides the driver's cab from the cargo area. I remember thinking this probably meant the truck had been used for some delivery the previous night which had fit in the back half of the trailer. I figured the delivery had been made late the previous evening and after the delivery, it was too late to go to the landfill. The Central Facility, I mean."

"But you said you used a dolly. Is there a dolly usually in the back of the truck trailer?"

"No. Not usually. I can't remember if I put a dolly in or not. But I did use the dolly to empty the trailer."

"So, the truck might have been used to transport some cargo while the stuff you offloaded was in the trailer?"

"Had to be. How long the junk was in there, I do not know."

"Was that unusual?"

"Nahh, not really. Well, in a way, yeah. If I was doing a normal run, not one to the hospital, there is no way of knowing ahead of time how large the load is. I mean, I just drive the truck. I go where I have the paperwork and take what is there to where I drop it off. It could be a full load or just a pallet. But when it comes to the hospital, pretty much every delivery is a full load."

"So, the load you took to the Central Facility that morning was unusual?"

"Out of the ordinary, yeah, but not unusual. I think I went to the hospital for more loads to the landfill that day. I don't know. It's hard to remember any one trip."

"I understand. Thanks for your memory?"

"Do you want some material on worker's rights?"

"Thanks. I'm good."

This tidbit was interesting but, as Noonan noted as he wrote Morgan's response in his notebook, it really didn't amount to much. Maybe the next call would be more productive.

It didn't start that way.

Sylvester Flynn, the security guard at the Hospital, was less than pleased Noonan reached him on his private cellphone.

Very much less than pleased.

"Noooo. Calling me at home! This is not what we agreed!"

"I know. I'm a bad boy. Just a few quick questions and I won't call you back."

"In a pig's eye."

"OK, maybe I'm lying. Now, the night you let in the Chugach Shipping truck, do you remember who was driving?"

"Not really. All I cared about was the paperwork. There are no names on the paperwork, just the manifest of what is being delivered."

"And as soon as you let them in, you left and went on our rounds?"

"Just like I told you."

"Do you remember anything about the person driving the truck?"

"White guy. In his forties. Maybe."

"You're not sure?"

"I'm not sure. A lot of the drivers are white men. I'd remember if it wasn't a white guy."

"Was he alone?"

"No, that I remember. Two other men. Natives."

"Young?"

"Not old. Forties. Dressed odd."

"Odd?"

"Jumpsuits. Not jeans and jackets. Thought it was odd. That's why I remember."

"Anything on the jumpsuits?"

"Like what?"

"Name of a company, logo, whatever."

"Not that I remember. And that's all I remember so don't call again!"

Then the iPhone in Noonan's hand went dead.

James Hayworth at the newspaper was friendlier. But then again, it would not be hard to find anyone more amiable than Sylvester Flynn had been.

"Captain!"

"Heinz."

"Not until the artifacts show up. I'm chomping at the bit for that story."

"You'll be the first to know."

"I hate it when you tease!"

"Just a couple of questions."

"It's gonna cost. You've got my phone number."

"That I do. I can't find much information on Jerome Hemmingway. Can you help me there?"

"Possibly, but not much. You've heard about the 'power behind the throne?' Well, Jerome is the guy *behind* the power behind the throne. Anything he is involved with is devious and six inches from the edge of the law. Highly competent and completely silent. An enigma in the true sense of the word."

"Have any background on him?"

"A little. But then again, he shies away from the limelight. Born during the Great Depression to working-class parents. Worked his way through college and law school. In the Bay Area. I think he grew up in San Jose when it was a small town. Was drafted and spent two years in the military, where I do not know. After he got out, he went to law school, Hastings in San Francisco, so he's pretty smart. He came to

Alaska in about 1967. My bet, he comes from a working-class family, and you need connections to make the big bucks in San Francisco and the Bay Area. So, he came north. To Fairbanks."

"Smart move."

"Better than that. He was in the right place at the right time. The pipeline boom was just starting and even more important for a law-yer, the Alaska Native Lands Claims Settlement Act passed in 1972. Suddenly he was the go-to lawyer for estates, trusts, wills, corporate documents whatever. Harrison Anderson's from Fairbanks so I'm sure they met there. They both went to Hastings so there's another bond – and I do not mean James." Hayworth chortled.

"How about the other names on the Board of Directors of the Aboriginal Artifact Commission? Do their names ring any bells?"

"Yeah, political parasites. Suits. Always looking for a quick buck with no work. Deeply involved in Native village politics. Legislator wan-na-be types. Would rather steal a nickel then earn an honest dime. They aren't felons, if that's what you're asking, just grafters."

"There's a possibility that Jerome pulled them in with Harrison Anderson for some scam with Aboriginal Artifact Commission?"

"I find it hard to believe they were **NOT** put on the Board except to drain grant money away from the Commission. They all have a high honorarium and lots of travel and per diem money. The Commission is a classic scam that is legal. You set up a nonprofit, collect grant money and donations, and then fail to deliver. There was so much money during the pipeline boom the feds only went after the very big boys and girls. Small fry walked free. It's a lot harder now."

"So, you think the Commission is into a scam?"

"I don't *think it*. I know it. It's only a matter of how and when. Unfortunately, it will probably be legal. If it is, the newspaper won't raise a peep. We only go after people who break the law, not people who bend the rules. That's why the scams keep working."

CHAPTER 32

Noonan and Bernice Whitcomb had to call ahead to get access to the utility corridor behind the staircase in the cathedral-like entryway to the Anchorage Municipal Hospital. One of the loose ends of the matter of the missing artifacts was the apparent link of the missing stairs in the staircase of the entryway. As Noonan knew from close examination of the installed replacement steps, the removal and replacement would have required workers to get on the backside of the cathedral-like entryway wall. Noonan wanted a look-see on the reverse side of the wall where the stair steps were attached.

What should have been a simple request was convoluted. The construction was ongoing, so permission was required from both the hospital administration and the construction supervising team. Though Noonan and Whitcomb had called ahead to say they were coming, it took a while for the request to move down the Hospital chain of command and the construction conglomerate before Elmore McCommon showed up.

Then things got treacherous.

Very treacherous.

To begin with, Elmore McCommon, the man supposedly sent to coordinate the opening of the hallway door to the backside of the staircase, was not a pleasant fellow by any stretch of the term.

Or imagination.

Further, first, he refused to meet with Bernice Whitcomb because she was not in his chain of command. Then he made a derogatory reference to her being a woman. That was an error as well. He followed that comment with a refusal to meet with Noonan because Noonan was not a local law enforcement official. From there, his recalcitrance both heightened and widened.

Then the conversation veered – both terms 'conversation' and 'veered' being grotesquely euphemistic – into a demand for a written document which McCommon stated precisely should be the equivalent, if not, an actual warrant.

Whitcomb was livid but professional. She stated she was about to file some manner of charges which Noonan knew would have no affect – or effect – and would only, in the end, make Whitcomb look bad. Second, Whitcomb was not in McCommon's chain of command so, unfortunately, he had a legitimate point there. But making a derogatory statement about a woman would, over the long run, be worse for him than Whitcomb. After all, McCommon might have been all of 25 or 26, and judging that he did not have a wedding ring, it was safe to say he would learn that lesson down the road. As Noonan often said, 'Never argue with your wife, your doctor or your attorney.'

McCommon had yet to learn that lesson.

In the depths of Noonan's cranial cortex, a distant gong chimed.

With regard to McCommon's refusal to speak to Noonan, the detective suggested 'there is an easy way and a hard way' to get the information Whitcomb and Noonan wanted. McCommon would comply – and grumble as much as he wanted – or Noonan would pull strings and get the Anchorage Police involved. That, Noonan assured McCommon, would be unfortunate as it would take a day out of McCommon's life – and paycheck – and make his life somewhat miserable as well as put a blemish on his employment record.

McCommon didn't quite 'get the message' the way it was intended so he said he'd 'call around' and see 'what's what.' He waved Noonan and Whitcomb aside so he could make a "confidential phone call." Then he advanced to the far side of the cathedral-like west entrance of the hospital and made a call.

Whitcomb was infuriated. "At least he didn't say anything about me being black."

Noonan snapped his fingers in front of her face. "It's a ruse, Bernice. We're being played. Now, I need you to do something for me right now. I don't have time to explain. Just do it. Call Regina Hemmingway right now. Keep her on the phone as long as you possibly can."

"I won't ask why. But what do I ask her?"

"Oh, ask her for any updates on the missing artifacts. Ask her if she has a timeline for when the artifact crates were loaded onto pallets. Thank her for the paperwork on the visits of Chugach Shipping to the landfill. Come up with anything else you can to keep her on the line. And keep looking angry at McCommon. I'll explain later."

With that Noonan walked slowly toward McCommon.

McCommon waved Noonan back.

Noonan looked back at Whitcomb who began talking to someone on her cell phone.

After several minutes, McCommon indicated Noonan should come to speak to him. "I have permission for *you* to look at the interior of the corridor. But," he pointed a finger at Whitcomb. "not her."

Noonan gave a Cheshire Cat smile. "I'm sure that will be all right."

Then Noonan walked over to Whitcomb who was still on the phone. When she saw Noonan give her a signal that she could hang up, she did.

"I have permission to visit the utility corridor. You don't."

Whitcomb was about to explode.

Noonan cut her off with a movement of the index finger of his right hand. "We are further along than you realize. Go to a coffee shop at least two miles from here and wait for me. Do not go back to your office and do not talk to anyone else before I get there. I'll call when I'm through here."

"Why a coffee shop? And why at least two miles from here?"

"Precaution. I'll give you a call when I'm through here."

Whitcomb left in a huff that was easy for McCommon to see. "Women!" he said and that seemed to sum up his attitude of Whitcomb. Then, to Noonan he said flatly, "My instructions are to let you see the wall of the utility corridor. That's it. Nothing else."

"Works for me."

McCommon led Noonan to a door at the side of the elevator shafts. He hunched over the door handle and tapped in the security code while looking over his right shoulder to make sure Noonan could not see the input. Then he pulled the door opened and indicated Noonan should enter the dark interior. When McCommon entered, he flicked on the overhead light.

The utility corridor extended about 20 feet along the right wall of the cathedral-like entrance. It was a wide hall, clearly a conversion from the old emergency room which had been on the ground floor of the west entrance. There were two doors that led to the elevator shafts and, against a distant wall, three other doors. One was open and revealed an office. The light was on, and Noonan could see a desk and some electronic screens against the back wall.

All Noonan was allowed was a glance. McCommon hurried Noonan along to a mobile frame the kind painters would use about ten feet from the door. Well above eye-level, Noonan could see a string of bolts leading upwards, clearly the bolts for the stairway on the other side of the wall. The painter's frame beneath the bolts.

"There you are," McCommon said without emotion. "Feel free to climb on the frame."

Noonan kind of nodded and let his eyes follow the string of bolt heads. "And the stairs are ship-shape now?"

"Never were anything else." Again, a flat tone.

Noonan pointed at the string of bolts, "Do you know which ones go to the stair steps that were missing?"

"Nope. Below my paygrade."

Noonan looked down the utility corridor. "Is this the only utility corridor in the building."

McCommon was silent for a long moment and then said, "My instructions were to let you see the bolt heads and only the bolt heads. Nothing else. No answers to any questions. Now, you've seen the bolt-heads. Is there anything else you want to see?"

Noonan gave a faux smile. "Nope, I'm good."

"Then *we* are out of here," he said with brutal emphasis on the word 'we.'

CHAPTER 33

When Noonan caught up with Whitcomb at the Alascattalo Café and Burger, she was ready to explode. Noonan let her stew for a few more minutes while he ordered a soft drink and an oatmeal cookie. It was after 11 in the morning, so Noonan knew to stay away from coffee, decaf or otherwise. When he finally sat down, Whitcomb blew steam.

"WHAT the …"

Noonan waved her silent. "Bernice, with all due respect, we are in a very different ball game today than we were in yesterday. Before we go on, let me give you three bits of advice to mull. First, anytime anyone says something to your face about being a woman, let it ride. For one of two reasons. One, the person is an idiot, and you don't want to spend your time arguing with a moron. Second, it is a way of throwing you off your game. When you are angry, you are not thinking. McCommon is not an idiot; he is a pawn in a ploy."

Noonan took a breath. "The second bit of advice is to never lose sight of the big picture. Everything is part of a big picture and the point of being a good cop," he pointed at her, "or an insurance investigator, is to see everything as a puzzle piece. Third, be proactive. Do not simply accept what is before you. Think about the angles you can play."

Whitcomb physically relaxed. "OK, I guess I know all of those reasons, but I am still frosted for being disparaged as a woman."

"Forget it. Just don't let it happen again. You are a competent person and when someone uses your sex as an insult, there is something else happening behind the scenes. Don't be fooled."

"Heard and agreed to. Now, what's going on?"

Noonan smiled and said softly, "Bernice! Good cops," he pointed at her, "and insurance investigators are jugglers. We take all the facts we have and juggle them into scenarios. Right now, we know for a fact the artifacts are gone. Missing, yes, not stolen. We know that because the artifacts have no value. Well, then where is the value? My guess, the paperwork with the artifacts. OK, and don't shake your head until you hear me out."

"I'm listening."

"You are doing what everyone else is doing. What the bad boys and girls want you to do. You are looking at the artifacts as the center of the problem. They are not. There is no money there. Where is the money? With the Aboriginal Artifact Commission? That's where the money collected and donated is sitting. The disappearance of the artifacts is a necessary distraction. Why, I do not know. At least not yet."

Whitcomb squinted as she thought. "If that's the case, why am I involved? My company insured the artifacts. We have nothing to do with any hanky-panky with money collected by the Aboriginal Artifact Commission."

"I agree. Had I not been dragged into this matter, here's what I think would have happened. You would be asked to pay for the artifacts and the actual amount of money to be paid and to whom would drag out for years. The loss of the artifacts would be no big deal because none of the museums had paid for them in the first place. So, the delay in getting the artifacts was no skin off their noses, so to speak. And they would be getting no money from the Aboriginal Artifact Commission so whatever money has been collected could be spent by the Commission searching," Noonan said and made quote marks in the air, "for the artifacts."

"But how did your getting involved change anything? The artifacts are still missing, and no money has been collected."

"Good question with no answer. A wild guess would be the bad people are doubling down on their security. I bet they are maneuvering with greater caution. Right now, nothing that has been done is illegal. No one has stolen the artifacts. No one has spent money authorized for the museum transfer. They are playing it very, very cool. Until I leave. Then the game goes, so to speak, 'back to normal' whatever that 'normal' was."

Whitcomb shook her head. "A lot of what you are saying I can see. But I'm still lost. Why did you want to see the back of the replaced stairs in the first place?"

"Those stairs are part of the grand scheme. Somehow, I do not know yet. They are circumstantial to the case. Chugach Shipping is involved. I am sure of it. It is just conveniently in too many places at the right time to be eliminated. Why the stairs are missing, I do not know. But when I came in contact with McCommon, I knew for sure I was on the right track."

"How's that. I saw everything you did. Or at least until I got the boot."

Noonan smiled. "If you were a rookie cop, I'd say something like 'listen and learn.' But you are not a cop and the chances of you ever being involved in a similar case are remote. But we're up to our eyebrows in this one so we have to lay all the cards on the table. Here's what I saw."

"I'm ready. Do I need to write this down?"

"Nope. Just remember the clues for the next time."

"Got it."

"You called ahead so there should have been no problems. But there were. That wasn't necessarily a clue, but it was odd."

"Why?"

"Hospitals are usually unbelievably competent when it comes to permissions. To be stalled after you called was odd. Including the construction team is routine but if there were nothing to hide, we would have been in and out in a matter of 15 or 20 minutes. But we had to wait an hour. Why? Not for permission to be granted, but for someone to figure out how to make sure we did not see something we were not supposed to see."

"Which was?"

"I have no idea. All I know is that we were stalled for some reason. Then, when you showed up, I am sure McCommon was told to upset you. Make you angry. Then they could use that as an excuse to get you to leave."

"That doesn't make any sense. Why should they, or anyone, be afraid of me?"

"My guess, I'm the outsider. I will only be here until my wife wants us to return to the Outer Banks. Dealing with me is easy. Just delay as long as possible and I will go home. You are a fly in the ointment. You are not going away, and you will only be involved in the matter of the missing artifacts until they turn up. The less you know upfront, the better for them."

"So why not just tell me to buzz off. They could, you know. I had no reason to look at the back of the replacement steps."

"You were with me. They, whoever they are, will assume we talk and share information."

"But I was with you at the hospital."

"My bet, you called and asked for permission to see the back of the replacement steps. I'm betting they assumed you were calling for me. I'm a nosey detective so let me have a look-see. Like I said before, I'll be gone in a week or two. But when you showed up, you were unexpected. McCommon tried the oldest trick in the book, insult a woman and hope she leaves in a huff. You didn't. So McCommon called for a Plan B."

"Who did he call?"

"Not a clue. But I know who he did *not* call?"

"Regina Hemmingway. I was on the phone with her."

"Correct. It's a bit of reverse thinking. Regina seems to fit everywhere. She owns Chugach Shipping. She is on the Board of the Aboriginal Artifact Commission. She is the niece of the man who created the non-profit organization to raise money for the museum transfer. Chugach Shipping is suspiciously present at the right time in the right places too many times to be coincidental. So, was she involved in what may very well be a plundering of the Aboriginal Artifact Commission?"

"Is she?"

"My bet, no. McCommon was on his cell phone asking for instructions. I told you to call Regin and keep her on the phone as long as possible. If Regina had been involved with the scam, she would have put you on hold or said she couldn't talk at the moment. She didn't. To me, that means she is out of the loop of whatever happens."

"Who's still in the loop?"

"Wild guess, her brother Johnathan. He has access to the trucks at Chugach Shipping so he can be anywhere he wants at any time. And with no paperwork to track his deliveries or what he picks up."

"But he can't load the trucks. He's one person."

"I agree. I think I know who the others are but it's the basic problem cops face. There's what we can prove and what we are sure of but cannot prove."

"I won't pry. But I will take your advice to heart. Next time someone gets rude I'll let it slide."

"Or make a joke of it. Humor has a way of defusing problems."

"I'll remember that." She sighed and took a gulp of coffee. "Couple of other things now that we are being so friendly. Why did you say to come here and not my office?"

"Again, a guess. McCommon was on the phone long enough for someone to get to the hospital. Why? To follow you. If you had gone back to your office, the bad boys and girls would have assumed you were going to call around and make trouble. There's also a possibility your phone is bugged. We could be talking several million dollars and they do not want you to upset any apple carts. When you came here, I'm betting they assumed you were just letting off steam. That's good news for them."

"You think they are out there now? In the parking lot?"

"Doubt it. The game was over when I got the boot from the utility corridor in the hospital. They knew there was nothing for me to see so they let me look. After I left and you were gone, they figured to be in the clear."

"Are they?"

"I can't prove anything."

"Well, what did you see they didn't want you to see?"

"Tidbits. McCommon used a code to get into the utility corridor. Inside I saw an open door with a desk inside and some screens. I'm betting that it's McCommon's desk and he's responsible for security surveillance. That would explain the surveillance failure Sylvester Flynn told us about."

"Does that mean the artifacts could be in the hospital?"

"Don't know. The artifacts were on pallets that were moved by a forklift. The doorway to the utility corridor is not wide enough for pallets and I didn't see any doorways inside that were wide enough for pallets. Besides that, there are witnesses who offloaded the pallets at the Anchorage Warehouse and Storage Facility."

Whitcomb shook her head. "Then why would anyone turn off the surveillance equipment to let someone unbolt and steal six stairsteps?"

"That, Ms Whitcomb, I do not know."

CHAPTER 34

One of the curses of law and order is the rat's nest of loose ends. Every case had lots of leads, but not every lead is important. Or critical. Many leads will remain loose ends after the crime has been solved. Or, were insignificant to begin with in regard to the big picture. But the problem with loose ends is the detective cannot tell ahead of time which loose end is important and which are simply a waste of time.

One of those loose ends was Jaron Flint, the bingle dealer. He had actually been in the National Bank of Anchorage Museum when the pairing of the archives with the provenances was done. Looking over his notes, Noonan was reminded that Flint had witnessed the crate of bingles loaded onto a pallet at the National Bank of Anchorage. So, talking with Flint was one of those loose ends.

Noonan, a seasoned interrogator, was also a skookum interviewer. Flint had introduced himself to Noonan with a joke, so Noonan was prepared to follow suit. As soon as Flint sat down in Bernice Whitcomb's office, Noonan hit him with a zinger.

"What do you call a rat with a wooden leg that steals your lunch?"

Flint loved it. "Let me see, a rat with a wooden that steals your lunch, humm." He thought for a good six seconds and admitted he did not know.

"A Pi-rat," Noonan said. All three burst into laughter.

"It's good to know cops have a sense of humor," Flint said as he stretched in his chair. "Now, what can do for the two of you? The artifacts are still missing so I'm guessing you are still on scent."

"Unfortunately," Noonan said as he shrugged, "you are correct." He smiled. "You are one of the few people who actually saw some of the packaging of artifacts so we'd," he indicated Whitcomb and himself, "like to know what you remember."

"Not much. It looked to me to be pretty routine. And competent, if you want to know the truth. Most of the bingles were in coin-sized cardboard displays, the way you'd see them in a coin store, with numbers on the cardboard. Johnathan Hemmingway would read the number and one of the Kagoona twins would get the archive paperwork."

Bingo!

The name Kagoona rang a bell.

Noonan remembered there was a Kagoona who was one of the Board members of the Aboriginal Artifact Commission. Noonan wasn't so much shocked as surprised. "Kagoona twins? The sons of a member of the Board of the Aboriginal Artifact Commission? You knew the Natives doing the archive work?"

"Well, no, I didn't know them. I knew *of them.* They are the twin sons of Henry Kagoona. Yeah, he's a Board member of the Commission. He ran for State Senate out of Fairbanks about three years ago. Lost. But his television ads had him with his two sons, twins, John and George. He's a mover and shaker in the Native community. He's also on the Board of the Aboriginal Artifact Commission. That's good news to someone like me because it means there are competent people handling the artifacts."

Noonan glanced at Whitcomb.

If she was surprised by the revelation, she did not show it.

"Interesting," was all Noonan could think to say. "Did Johnathan Hemmingway know the twins were the sons of an Aboriginal Artifact Commission Board member?"

"Not that I care," Flint said. "I find it hard to believe he *did not* know. Not that it makes any difference. A Board member pulling strings to get his sons work is not unknown. The Native community in Alaska is small so I'm not surprised the twins were working there."

"I was told Jonathan and his sister grew up in Fairbanks. Could the twins have known Johnathan from there?"

"Probably. Like I said, the Native community is small. Smaller when you focus on Fairbanks."

"I see," Noonan opened his notebook. "Now, as you were watching the loading of the pallet was there anything unusual. You know, out of place?"

"*Everything* was unusual. I have never seen a museum being dismantled. If you mean was the scene disorganized, no. The three of them knew what they were doing, and it was down to a routine. There was no fumbling with the artifacts. Did I see artifacts lying around waiting to be packed? No. I did not see any artifacts. What I did see were boxes wrapped in plastic with paper labels and envelopes on top. I'm assuming the envelopes contained the provenances. Except, of course, in the case of the coins. Coins do not have provenance which is why I was watching them with an eagle eye."

"So, nothing was out of place."

"A professional job, not that I know how a museum should be dismantled. But, in answer to your cop question, I saw nothing suspicious. In fact, I saw the opposite. It was a smoothly running operation."

Noonan closed his notebook. "Well, thanks for stopping by."

"Not a problem," Flint said as he stood up. "Since you like jokes so much, if you hit a rat with your car, what do you write on the accident report?"

"Rat jokes, OK. Let me think. Now, I don't know."

"*Road dent.*"

CHAPTER 35

As soon as Flint left, Noonan asked Whitcomb if she knew the twins were the ones working on packaging the artifacts.

"No, but I'm not surprised. Having Natives work on Native artifacts is a good idea. That they are children of a Board member doesn't surprise me. Grease on the wheel."

Noonan smiled. "Same the world around. What do you know about Henry Kagoona?"

"Just what Flint said," Whitcomb tilted her head toward the door of her office. "He ran for State Senate in Fairbanks and lost. His television ads were dull, like most political ads, and I remember his sons. He talked about the need to have a Native perspective in the State Legislature. I don't think the Aboriginal Artifact Commission was in existence then."

"What does he do for work?"

"Investments, if I remember correctly. Banking and real estate. Had to be a mover and a shaker in the Native community to make it to the Board of the Aboriginal Artifact Commission. Nothing else. No sticky fingers or, at least, nothing that made the papers."

Noonan plowed through his notes and found the page he was looking for. "According to the internet, the Aboriginal Artifact Commission has four Board members. There's Harrison Anderson and Regina

Hemmingway. Now there's Henry Kagoona. Do you know who the other one is?"

"No. Is it important?"

"At this stage of the game, sort of."

"Give me a moment." Whitcomb punched up the Aboriginal Artifact Commission and her computer. "The fourth one is Steven Salinas. Let's see what else I can find." She diddled on the computer for a few minutes and then punched for a printout. When the printer spit out the copy, she handed it to Noonan.

"Not much. Another Fairbanks mover and shaker. No way of knowing if he is a Native. Has his fingers in many pies. Started as a pilot back in the bad old days and is still in the transportation business."

Noonan heard a dull clang in his cerebral cortex. "Transportation? As in people or cargo?"

"Same thing in Alaska. I didn't see he had anything to do with trucking so I'm betting it's all air cargo. A lot of that into Fairbanks and to the remote villages of the bush."

"But only in Fairbanks?" Noonan said suspiciously.

Whitcomb gave Noonan the 'I know what you're thinking' look. "No, I did not find any link on the internet that he has any involvement with the Hemmingways, Chugach Shipping or the Anchorage Warehouse and Storage Facility. But,..." she let the sentence hang.

"Let me guess," Noonan said with a twisted smile, "there is a lot of cargo going to the Anchorage Municipal Hospital so it's a good bet Salinas has business links in Anchorage."

"That," Whitcomb said with a wicked smile, "is an understatement."

CHAPTER 36

Noonan and Whitcomb had no problem reaching Lael Morgan, the shipping temp who had made the trips to the landfill for Chugach Shipping. But she was working and said she'd call back. It took more than an hour for her to return the call.

"Socialism is still the key to the future. Gotta pay workers more. Tax the rich and businesses. Way of the world. More money to the working class and the more they will spend. It's historical."

"I'm sure that's the case," Noonan said as he looked sideways at Whitcomb. "The way of the world."

Whitcomb's face was noncommittal.

"We wanted to ask you a few more questions if you don't mind."

"Shoot, Luke."

"Who actually calls you to work for Chugach Shipping?"

"No one. I get the call from the Teamsters, and I show up."

"Do the Teamsters put you on a list and you get a job in some kind of order of priority?"

"Not really. Chugach Shipping likes me, so I usually get the call from them to make sure I'm available. Then the Teamsters call. I don't know how that works, administratively. I like working for Chugach Shipping and they clearly like me."

"OK," Noonan was writing in his notebooks, "and when you show up for work, who do you check in with?"

"Johnathan. He's responsible for the actual work. His sister is stuck in the office. I've only seen her on the garage floor maybe two times. Johnathan is in charge of everything in the garage and storage area."

"Have you ever been in the storage area?"

"All the time. Chugach Shipping is small so sometimes they combine loads. Particularly if the delivery is in Fairbanks. Unless it's a rush, they wait until they have a full load before sending a truck north."

"How long would they wait?"

"Day or two. Not a week, if that's what you're asking."

"No," Noonan said as he looked at Whitcomb. "I'm assuming most of the shipping for Chugach is in Anchorage."

"It is. I think I've only taken one trip to Fairbanks in the last year. Soldotna, Seward and once to Homer. But right now, the loads are from the Anchorage Warehouse and Storage Facility to the hospital."

"And to the landfill," Noonan hinted.

"Oh, yeah. To the landfill. I'm making good money with Chugach Shipping. Don't mess it up."

Noonan laughed. "Not a chance." He flipped through his notebook. "The last time we spoke, you said that when you went to the landfill, there were people there who unloaded the truck trailer."

"Right."

"But when you went to the Central Facility, you did the offloading."

"Right."

"When you went to the Central Facility, what kind of stuff did you offload?"

"Small stuff. I mean, the big loads were going to the landfill. The smaller loads go to the Central Facility. Lots of ripped-up cardboard boxes, damaged shipping containers, occasionally broken furniture, and sheets of plastic."

"Sheets of plastic?"

"Yeah, you know. When you have loaded a pallet, you wrap it with a plastic sheet. That stabilizes the load."

"How often did you offload plastic sheets?"

"Not that often. There was a rush of them a while back and then nothing."

"Anything else appear in a rush?"

"Not really. The bulk of the stuff going to the Central Facility comes from the hospital. I arrive and there's a pile. We load it and off I go."

"When the plastic sheets were loaded inside your trailer, was that at the hospital?"

"Not that I remember, at the Chugach Shipping garage."

The clang in Noonan's cerebral cortex was now distinctive.

CHAPTER 37

Whitcomb leaned back in her chair and stared across the desk at Noonan. "You know, Heinz, I'm not in the law-and-order business. I mean, I'm the type of woman who pays for an hour of parking just in case my ten minutes isn't ten minutes. But now I'm in a crime story right up to my eyebrows. I think I've got all the evidence you've got, and I'm still lost."

Noonan chuckled. "What makes you think I know what's going on?"

"You'd better because I'm lost."

Noonan chuckled again. "Being a detective is just like being the person on the street. Forget what you think you learned from television and Sherlock Holmes movies. It does not matter what you think or, for that matter, what you can prove. It's what a group of 12 people who know nothing about law-and-order think. What they will accept as true. And right now, as they say in California, we have zip."

Whitcomb was in agony. "Zip?! The case is not coming together! All we know is a group of people is pulling a fast one with artifacts and we don't know why!"

Noonan waggled the index finger of his right hand. "Bernice, we've got a lot of facts with nowhere to go. Yes, there appears to be a group of people who have orchestrated the disappearance of artifacts. But we can't prove a crime. Just that the artifacts are missing. And there is no logical reason for the artifacts to be missing. Furthermore, and unfortunately, we cannot prove there is a dime to be made in selling the artifacts. Until we can prove an artifact has been sold and we can trace it back to the National Bank of Anchorage Museum, we have nothing."

"But we know,…"

"We know nothing criminal. Yes, it appears there is a despicable action afoot, but there is no crime. No crime means no arrest. Worse, particularly from my point of view, there is no money involved. When it comes to a crime of passion, like murder, you can find the perp, er, perpetrator quickly. The problem is not finding the perp, it's proving he or she did it. Finding a money trail helps but you still must have the forensics, the witness statements, and the errors made in the commission of the crime to trip up the perp. When it comes to crimes that do not involve passion, you follow the money. Right now, we do not have a clue where the money is."

"Not true," Whitcomb snapped. "We know there was a lot of money collected with the nonprofit when it was trying to save the museum. That was cash. Where's that cash?"

"Good try," Noonan said as he shook his head. "That money was earmarked for the museum before it went under. When the museum went under, the money went to the Aboriginal Artifact Commission. It's all on paper, rather, on the record. If someone wanted to dip into the till and take any of the money, there is going to be a paper trail. How much money is there, I do not know. But it is accounted for, and it will be very hard to walk away with any of that cash without going to jail. I see the money you are talking about, but I do not see how anyone is going to dip into the till and not get caught. You can follow the money and the IRS is very good at catching people who do."

"So where are we?"

Noonan grimaced. "I know you will not like this, but we are back where we started. We are still missing the artifacts; the nonprofit money is secured and everyone who is probably a bad person has all the cards. Right now, the best we can do is wait a bit and see what happens next."

CHAPTER 38

Flail is the worst word in a detective's vocabulary. It's a 'word' which has no real-world equivalent. When used by a sports broadcaster, for example, the term implies a condition where one team or contestant seems to have lost his/her/their bearing and is striking out because "he/she/they has/have to do something." It is also a prescription for disaster. Flailing means you are trying anything and everything in the hopes that something will work.

But – and this is a significant 'but' – when used as a sport term, there is an end in sight. All sporting contests in which one could be flailing have a finality. You can always 'come back next time' to 'do better than we did this time' but that is in sports. Not law-and-order. To 'flail' in the law-and-order world has no finality. There are a lot of reputation-savings expressions to describe that finality. There is 'not a priority at this time,' 'we are still following leads,' and 'there are events in motion which will take some time to apply to what we already know.' But, in fact, the flail is the last moment before the matter has another term: cold case.

Noonan was flailing.

He had lots of loose ends but the possibility of any one of them leading to finality was remote. This was primarily because there had yet to be a crime to resolve. There was not a single determining clue to suggest the artifacts had been stolen. Further, even if stolen, there was no reasonable explanation. At best, if the artifacts were sold, they might return a few thousand dollars. Even at ten thousand dollars, it was not worth anyone's time to leap through the felonious hurdles to sell the artifacts. And it would only take the discovery of one artifact to bring the entire enterprise to the attention of the police.

Further, there did not seem to be a way to take legal advantage of any of the money from either the saving of the National Bank of Anchorage Museum or the formation of the nonprofit to distribute the artifacts after the museum was deemed to be defunct. Money is easy to trace, and the penalties are set in stone.

So, what was going on?

CHAPTER 39

W hen you do not know what to do but have to do something, go back to ground zero. If there is no ground zero, you go back to the place where you think ground zero is. For Noonan, the only place that had potential was the Anchorage Municipal Hospital. The other locals were solid zeros. Yes, there had been a delivery to the Anchorage Warehouse and Storage Facility. What happened to the pallets inside was not yet known. And, the delivery to the Anchorage Warehouse and Storage Facility had been made by Chugach Shipping. Noonan was not a betting man but, if he were, he guessed the original boxes and crates of artifacts from the National Bank of Anchorage Museum had made it to the Chugach Shipping garage and warehouse. Most likely what was supposedly to have been on the pallets that were delivered to the Anchorage Warehouse and Storage Facility were not those artifacts. It had been another shipment with museum paperwork. There, paperwork was probably switched so the artifacts 'disappeared.' Why was not yet clear, and who could have done it was unknown, but that, in Noonan's experience, was the most likely scenario. Step One of some nefarious deed.

So where were the artifacts?

Logically, they were somewhere in the Anchorage Municipal Hospital. Chugach Shipping was in and out of the western entrance on an ongoing basis so it would have been easy to smuggle the artifacts in. Most likely, the crates and boxes of artifacts on the six pallets would be removed and brought into the hospital a box or crate at a time with a dolly. Again, it would have been easy to bring in boxes of any description because all manner of building material was being brought into the hospital for renovation. It would seem logical that the boxes of artifacts were taken upstairs to some room under construction and hidden in a wall. Why, Noonan did not know. It would have been easy enough. The only security camera that appeared to have been tampered with was on the ground floor of the western entrance and he only knew that because Elmore McCommon had been hiding something. Also, the missing stairs had come from the ground floor. Could the artifacts be on the ground floor and not secreted in some upstairs cubby hole?

Even more important, why were the artifacts missing in the first place?

The Anchorage Municipal Hospital was the logical place to start. Noonan placed a call to Bernice Whitcomb and asked if she was available for another look at the hospital. She said fine, but not today. That left Noonan with a whole day to come up with another approach.

His choice was the internet. His last search had been scanty, but that had been because he didn't have all the names then he had now. So, he went through his notebook and listed every name he had. Then he went methodically about the search. Every name was punched into court records, probate filing, land ownership lists, corporation indexes and newspaper archives – along with random searches on the internet.

In all professions and, as a matter of fact, in all lives, there are required functions called 'the grind.' It is the proverbial sifting through haystacks looking for a pin which may or not be there. Lawyers read through piles of legal cases looking for the one tidbit that will turn a case around. Historians plumb the depths of government records, diaries, newspaper archives and letter collections looking for the one document that would make a dull scholarly book a best seller. There may – or may not – be nuggets of gold in the dump truck loads of chaff but you will never know until you looked. It's well-known that only 10% of all argonauts who came north during the Alaska Gold Rush became wealthy. But a lot made enough money to take a steamship home. So, that 10% is a misleading statistic. Only 10% of all Americans will rise above their station and become wealthy but many will earn enough to be comfortable and above the station they were born in. Luck is a large part of success, but the fact of the matter is summed up in the adage that the harder you work the luckier you get.

Thus did Noonan begin the grind. But there was a saving grace. In the *ancient* times, those days before the internet, research meant perambulating from archive to library to courthouse to document repository just to find the chaff. Now the raw material was a mouse click away and, with each passing day, more and more of the chaff and the hidden nuggets of information are available from your desktop computer.

Noonan started with the easiest electronic depository: probate records. He got nothing. Then he moved on to court files, criminal records first. Only three names popped up: Jerome Hemmingway, William Chambers and Steven Salinas. But all were nonstarters. Hemmingway had been charged with some manner of document mismanagement and the case was dismissed quickly after it had been filed. For Chambers it was a charge he had received 'stolen property' and was part of an ongoing campaign by a Native group trying to get aboriginal items for a museum it wanted to open. Noonan had never heard of the museum, and it was not on the internet which was a good indication the institution had never made it off the ground. There were a number of cases against Salinas, but they were all because he was one of the owners of a number of businesses who were being charged with violations of environmental regulations, sexual harassment allegations and, interestingly, unsafe labor conditions at the Anchorage Warehouse and Storage Facility. That linked Salinas to the warehouse. All cases were closed. The civil court files were packed with cases involving his name. The bulk of them were for collections, small claims, and failure to meet deadlines for governmental requirements. One was a cease-and-desist case against Lael Morgan for passing out "Socialist and union literature without a parade permit, littering and loitering." A quick look at the case revealed Morgan was one of 15 people who had been arrested for nonviolently protesting a garbage collection company. The case was ten years old, and Noonan could not find the name of the garbage collection company, so he assumed it was no longer in business. George and John Kagoona had a laundry list of misdemeanors including several each with DUIs, some disturbing the peace, resisting arrest, speeding, parking violations, and drunk driving arrests. All were in Fairbanks and all had been dismissed.

Land records were, at the very least, informative in the sense most of the names showed up as mortgage holders for homes. None of them into the millions. With one exception. Jerome Hemmingway had, at one time, well over a million dollars in mortgages which, over the years, had received deeds of reconveyance. This meant the mortgage had been paid off. There was no indication as to the ownership of the property at that moment. This was of particular interest to Noonan because a State of Alaska requirements for residence in the Senior Home for Pioneers was to have no assets. So those assets must have gone somewhere. He found them when he pulled up the property listings for Regina and Johnathan Hemmingway. Checking dates, it appeared all properties had been transferred on the same day – presumably just before Jerome had entered the Senior Home for Pioneers. Interesting, there was no record for property mortgaged by William Chambers. The man was wealthy enough to fund the National Bank of Anchorage Museum out of his own pocket but owned no home? Odd.

The business and corporation records did not reveal much of interest. Regina was listed as the owner of Chugach Shipping; Johnathan was not listed. Chambers was the sole owner of the Chambers Museum. The Chambers Museum was not listed as a nonprofit but as a business with one owner, William Chambers. The Anchorage Warehouse and Storage Facility had nine names listed as corporation officers/owners, one of them being Steven Salinas. The National Bank of Anchorage had a long list of corporate officers, none of which appeared on Noonan's list of names being researched. Searching the nonprofit records, Noonan found every name he expected to be there.

Pulling up local newspaper indexes, Regina Hemmingway was revealed to be a prominent social activist. She donated to a plethora of social causes and nonprofits. She gave free shipping services to a wide range of charitable organizations and had a wall of certificates of merit. Johnathan was not mentioned in any newspaper article. Harrison Anderson had been invisible until the formation of the Aboriginal Artifact Commission. Then he became a frequent guest speaker at a spread of social service conventions and meetings, sometimes with Regina Hemmingway. William Chambers was rarely mentioned until he died and thereafter, he was only mentioned as 'the former owner of the museum on the ground floor of the National Bank of Anchorage.' Noonan could not find one mention of the "Chambers Museum."

Henry Kagoona, on the other hand, was a media star. Born in Shishmaref, he was recognized early on as a staggeringly bright individual. The local Quaker church was able to find foster parents for him in Fairbanks to attend elementary school. When he reached the 9th grade, he was admitted to the Sherman Institute in Riverside, California, considered the cream of the best off-reservation Native high school in the country. The Institute had been in operation since the 1890s and graduates went on to lustrous careers in all fields. After graduating from the Sherman Institute, Kagoona was admitted to the University of Alaska Fairbanks where he had a double major in business and English. He spoke four languages, English, the Native dialect of Shishmaref, French and Spanish.

He moved quickly into the private sector where he excelled in banking and investments. What made him such a standout was his ability to bridge the gap between Natives and non-Natives. Carefully stated in the newspapers, it was clear to Noonan what 'that' meant. Having married an Alaskan, Noonan understood there were Natives that businesses had to hire to show diversity. Often those Natives were not hired for their abilities. Kagoona had been hired for his ability and he shot to fame and fortune on his own merits. He was well into the millions when he set up his own investment company. Then the Alaska Native Claims Settlement Act passed in 1972. Overnight his ability to broker deals went to skyrocket. By then he was married to a Gwitchen woman from Fort Yukon and had two sons, twins, John and George.

By 2010, things appeared to take a downturn for Henry Kagoona. Being a Native financier in the previous decade had been a benefit because there were so few of them in the upper echelons of financial society. By 2010, they were a dime a dozen and many of them were as competent as Kagoona. Worse, there was what was quietly known as the 'Native hangover effect' of the Alaska Native Claims Settlement Act. The legislation had given Alaskan Natives about a billion dollars and 44 million acres of land, but it had extinguished all aboriginal rights. This had absolutely no affect at all on the Regional Native Corporations which continued to flout being Native to get lucrative and, many times, sole source no-bid contracts. But the money the corporations were making primarily went to those in the upper echelons of the corporations. A meager amount trickled down to the shareholders.

But the real impact of the 'Native hangover effect' was on the public. A large percentage of the homeless, drug-addicted, alcoholic individuals on the street in Alaskan communities were Natives. The financial responsibility for picking up and caring for these individuals was shouldered by the communities. This infuriated the tax-paying residents because every dollar spent on handling a homeless Native was one less dollar for local schools, libraries, police, and fire. The attitude of the Regional Corporations was that their function was to make money and what happened on the streets was not their concern. Or expense.

This attitude apparently played a huge part in the election – and loss – of Henry Kagoona when he campaigned for State Senate. His not-so-subtle message to the voters was that he would bring a "Native perspective" to the State Legislature. This was the wrong message to voters who were concerned about increased funding for schools, abortion, homelessness, drunk drivers, inflation, expanding public library hours and more money for the University of Alaska. Worse, Henry Kagoona highlighted his twin sons as "the next generation of leaders" which the voters interpreted as a continuation of the same exploitation by Regional Native Corporations voters were quietly complaining about. Midway through the campaign the concept of racism came up which, in Alaska, was laughable when 20% of the population was Native. But it was brought up and the undercurrent did not help Kagoona, and he was not elected.

A few months after his loss, Kagoona, Salinas and Harrison Anderson formed the Aboriginal Artifact Commission. It was set up as a nonprofit and initially funded by a coalition of Regional

Native Corporations. This was made clear by the several articles in which Anderson emphasized that Regional Corporation support was 'only for startup operations.' There was a portrait shot of the Board which Noonan reprinted. YouTube was next. Noonan found copies of Kagoona's State Senate commercial which he downloaded onto his Mephistophelian beast and then looked for footage of the Aboriginal Artifact Commission. He found one which he also downloaded on his cell phone. He could not find any YouTube shot of Johnathan Hemmingway or Jerome Hemmingway, but he did find a grainy image of Johnathan. It wasn't much but it was all he had. As far as Jerome was concerned, there wasn't so much of a mention of him on the internet. He was truly a 'behind the scenes' character. There were no YouTube clips of Steven Salinas, William Chambers or Elmore McCommon.

CHAPTER 40

"What are you doin' here?! It's ten o'clock at night! I'm on duty you know!"

Sylvester Flynn was more than displeased when he came down from his duty station on the Fifth Floor of the Municipal Hospital to speak with Noonan. "Being security means security, you know. I'm not doing security talking with you. You don't have anything better to do at ten o'clock at night than come here?!"

"Wish I did," Noonan said soothing the irate security guard. "I just need you to look at some pictures."

"What?!"

"Just a quick look. Then, I promise, I will not be back."

"Right! I've heard that before! Come on, make it quick!

Noonan showed him the grainy shot of Johnathan Hemingway. "The night the security system went on the fritz, was this the person who was driving the truck?"

"That's a lousy picture of the guy driving the truck. I'm security upstairs so I don't see the deliveries downstairs during the day."

Then Noonan opened up the YouTube download on his electronic Beelzebub and showed Flynn the political advertisement for Henry Kagoona with his two sons. "Were these the men helping Johnathan Hemmingway?"

Flynn pointed to one. "Him, yes, I got a good look at him. The other one, I don't know."

"Thanks!"

"Next time you come," Flynn said with a laugh, "bring a chicken sandwich."

CHAPTER 41

"Let me get his right, you are a Captain in the Sandersonville, North Carolina Police Force and you are doing *what* here in Anchorage?"

"It's a long story, Reverend. You are a reverend, yes?"

"Charles works better. I'm available when I am needed."

"At the Anchorage Municipal Hospital, correct?"

"Y-e-e-s-s. Why do you want to know?"

"I'm not sure if you know it, but artifacts from the old, now defunct, National Bank of Anchorage Museum are missing."

"I've heard that, Captain, it's …"

"Heinz. Until there's a crime, I'm just Heinz."

"Well, I'm just Charles. Anchorage is a small town, Heinz. Everyone knows the artifacts are missing. There's no crime here because artifacts have no value. Well, that is, they have a value in a museum but not as something you could pawn."

Noonan chuckled. "Well, you got that right."

"Again, Capt, er, Heinz, why the interest in the chapel at the Anchorage Municipal Hospital? And it's not a chapel. It's a Room of Repose. It's for people of any religious faith who need a few minutes of silence because of what has happened to their loved ones."

"I'm helping in the search for the artifacts."

"They aren't in the Room of Repose."

"I already guessed that, Charles. I just wanted to know if there has been any change in the room because of the construction. I mean, the chapel is right next to the elevator shafts and close to where the stairs were missing."

"I'm aware of the missing stairs. It's kind of a joke. I mean, really, why would anyone steal stairs?"

"That, Charles, I do not know. But, the way you put it, yes, it is rather funny."

"It's a hoot! Now, as far as the Room of Repose is concerned, the size has been changing for years. Every few years. It's sort of 'free space' so to speak when it comes to the hospital. You see, it, the hospital, needs a Room of Repose for those difficult moments in lives."

"So, the Room of Repose has not been reduced in size during the latest renovations?"

"Not really. We were moved out during the installation of the second elevator shaft and now we're back in. The room is still the same size."

"How do you know that for sure?"

"All the furniture still fits. The construction crews needed us to move out because the cable network has to be at ground level."

"Ground level?"

"Yes. The old elevator shaft allowed patrons to enter the hospital at ground level at the western entrance. That meant the elevator lift mechanism – or whatever it is called – had to be below ground level. But the new elevator box that carries people starts at the eastern entrance. That's a good 30 feet above the ground at the western entrance. That means all of the cable lift mechanism for the new elevator is at ground level at the western entrance. The elevators, as in the actual boxes people ride up to the floor where they need to go, do not get to the ground floor on the western side. When the new elevator shaft was put in, the Room of Repose was moved to an empty room in the back of the ground floor. Where the old Emergency Room used to be. Now that the new elevator is in service, the Room of Repose is back in service.

"But the room is still the same size?"

"The furniture fits so, yes, it's the same size. It would take a lot of space to hide those artifacts, I'm told. That's a lot of square footage. Even if we did lose footage, it would have been on the elevator shaft side. Even if our room was moved a few feet to store those artifacts, those feet would have had to have been made up by taking more square feet from the room next to the Room of Repose. That didn't happen."

"How do you know that?"

"Because its far wall is the side of the hallway. Pallets are, what four or five feet square. There's no way you could take that amount of square footage from the Room of Repose and the adjacent room and not have the missing square footage noticeable."

Noonan chuckled. "You read me like a book."

CHAPTER 42

Noonan had taken a day off to be with in-laws which, in Noonan's world, meant cavorting with many people he only knew through stories that may or not be true. One of his favorites which, truth be told, Noonan used but transposed someone else's experience for his own, was the day 'he' saw an "unidentified flying object." As the original story was told, an in-law was tired of passing out candy on Halloween. He wanted to go to bed but not deny children the candy he was afraid he would be eating for the next week if it wasn't given away. So, he did what many others do: he put what was left of his candy in a bowl on the front porch and then turned out the home's interior lights so he could go to bed and not be bothered by the doorbell ringing.

The first floor of the house went dark and, as he was passing through the kitchen, he glanced out the back window of his home which overlooked a game reserve. There, hovering over the wetlands, was a long, cylindrical object with what appeared to have Cyrillic lettering beaming down on the swampland. The individual in question immediately identified the object as a UFO. Instantaneously thereafter he realized there were no UFOs. Then, in the next nanosecond, he realized that even if it were a UFO, no one would ever believe him because he was a known prankster. As he marveled at the cylindrical object hovering over the wetlands, he saw the Cyrillic lettering change! Only then did he realize

THE MATTER OF THE HIJACKED ARTIFACTS

what he was viewing was the clock on the microwave which, in the dark room, was being reflected on the double-thick kitchen window!

But wait!

He thought he could pull a fast one!

He ran upstairs and urged his wife to come downstairs and "See the UFO with Cyrillic lighting hovering over the game reserve!"

His wife would have none of that. "You probably saw a reflection of the clock in the microwave on the kitchen window."

So much for pulling a fast one.

That was the way Noonan felt when it came to the missing artifacts. It was an illusion. The truth was there for everyone to see but he wasn't everyone. It was not as if he were looking at the pieces of a jigsaw puzzle scattered on the tabletop. That was too easy. He actually loved jigsaw puzzles because every piece fit, and a complete picture would be revealed. That was not the reality in law-and-order cases. You were always and only looking at the 'pieces,' so to speak, that you could see. You could guess at the others. In this case, the matter of the missing artifacts, he had a bit of an advantage. There was no crime involved. When a crime is involved, there is more than the discovery of the perpetrator involved. You have to be meticulous in both the discovery of evidence and the preserving of the chains of circumstances. That is, you had to solve the crime and then you had to make sure you had all the evidence needed to get a conviction. It did you no good to catch the perpetrator and have him, her or them, skate on justice. It did happen but not that often. By the time a case went to trial, the attorneys were pretty sure they had the case wrapped up.

He was contemplating his lack of progress on the discovery of the artifacts when one of his in-laws, a man whose face he recalled but whose name was a blank, waved him over to an empty spot on the seating slab of the picnic table. Noonan was pleased someone was *pleased* to see him, so he sat down.

"Tough day on the law-and-order treadmill," the man said and introduced himself as Elvis Kern. "No reason to remember me, Heinz. And, yes, my parents were a fan of Elvis."

"No surprise there," Noonan said. "Nice to have a day off, so to speak."

"Evil never sleeps," Kern said with a smile. "I'm glad I chose a dull, dull, dull profession."

"Which was?"

"Freelance technical writer. We're the invisibles. We do our job, and no one knows who we are."

"Oh?"

"See, a decade ago, when both of us were teenagers," he said as he laughed, and Noonan gave him a thumbs up. "A decade ago, all companies had writers on staff. Then along came the internet and the writers became contractors. Then freelancers. Everyone thinks they are a writer. I mean, after all, everyone has a computer so, *ta-dah!,* they are writers."

"Well, you know, anyone can get paints and a canvas so that must make them Rembrandt."

"Good parallel. Yeah, Rembrandts. Or Picassos. But the job of a freelance technical writer is actually very, very, good and verrrry bad at the same time. If you like people, it is bad. Technical writers work in an office and people throw documents at them and say, 'write it up!' I could be very happy as a hermit, so I love my job. I sit in an office and do my job, and no one bothers me."

"Sometimes I feel that way."

"I'll bet. Like right now. Everyone's watching you to see if you can find the *missing* artifacts." Kern waved his hands at shoulder level as if he were calling for help.

"Everybody seems to know that."

"Not really. Those of us in the loop do. I just happen to know a lot about what is going on in the Native community because I do grant writing for Native nonprofits. It's a small world and everyone talks about what Kagoona is going to do next."

"Really? Why?"

"Short story, actually. Man made a killing in the 1960s and 1970s when he was the only topflight Native wheeler-dealer. By 1980, the field was crowded. He was still wealthy, but his clients fled. By 2010, he should have retired to the Bahamas or wherever. But no, he didn't. Started chasing smaller and smaller fish. Had two loser kids so maybe he needed the money."

"So, he's not into the big bucks anymore?"

"Not the way he used to be. He's still a multi-millionaire but, you know, some people just can't quit. And he's associated with Jerome Hemmingway. Now there's an interesting fellow."

Noonan's legal antenna went up. "Jerome Hemmingway. Quite a character. He has Alzheimer's now."

"Doubt it. It's probably part of some scheme."

"Illegal?"

"Naw. Jeremy doesn't do illegal things. Just devious. You know, the people who advise on changing the law have already figured out a way around the reforms they are working on. Jerome has had a finger in every pie in Alaska since he got here."

"Fairbanks, right?"

"Started there. Married a Native woman, adopted her nephew and niece, Regina and Johnathan."

"Good people?" Noonan was a master at fishing.

"Regina, yeah. Top of the line. Everyone has good things to say about her. Does not have a crooked bone in her body. Has her finger-prints on every social, civic, progressive issue in Alaska. Lots of money courtesy of Jerome. Her brother, Johnathan, is a moron."

"Crooked?"

"Don't know. Hasn't been caught yet. Lazy."

Noonan knew it was time to go fishing. "Regina's on the Board of the Aboriginal Artifact Commission. A reputable association?"

"Haven't heard it isn't. Regina on the Board?"

"Yup. With guys named Harrison Anderson, Steven Salinas and Henry Kagoona. Know anything about them?"

"Harrison Anderson is a shill, a bottom feeder. If there is money, he is there. Has, what we Alaskans call, 'a flexible value system.' Do something illegal, probably not. But right to the edge of the law, yup. He linked up early with Jerome Hemmingway back in the 1970s and has done well for himself. Steven Salinas, nope, not a clue. Kagoona, yeah, everyone knows he's a self-promoter."

"The kind of a guy who'd dig into the till?"

"Not the way you mean it. I, we, everyone suspected he was running for State Senate to grease wheels. That's the Alaskans way of saying adjusting the law and regs to allow someone to make big bucks. Then, some of those big bucks would filter back. Sleazy, yes. Disreputable, yes. But doing something criminal, I doubt it."

"Any idea who he might have cut a deal with when he ran for public office?"

"No. But if you are clever, there's a way to find out."

"Really, how?"

"You're not from up here, Heinz. See, if you run for public office there are all kinds of paperwork requirements – including who gives you money. It's all public. Check with the APOC, the Alaska Public Office Commission. On the web. Everything is on the web now. Just pull it and maybe you'll find something interesting."

"I might just do that."

CHAPTER 43

The next morning, Noonan rose at the break of dawn which, in Alaska, in July, is in what everyone else in America calls the afternoon. Before he could search the internet for the Alaska Public Office Commission, he saw Bernice Whitcomb had called.

At the real break of dawn.

"Let me guess, the artifacts have been found."

"Not quite. We have a two o'clock meeting with Harrison Anderson. He is not a happy man."

"Uh, huh. Which means we are close to finding the artifacts. Are you up for some verbal abuse?"

"I was raised in a large family."

"Good answer. By the way, I found footage of Henry Lagoona's State Senate campaign advertisement."

"With the two sons?"

'Right. I showed them to Sylvester Flynn, the security guard at the hospital. He identified one of them as being with Johnathan Hemmingway during that late-night run when the security system went down."

"No surprise there."

"I also talked to the reverend who users the Room of Repose .."

"The what?"

"Room of Repose. It's the chapel-like room next to the new elevator shaft. I wanted to know if he lost any space, like maybe the artifacts were secreted in the wall of his Room of Repose. He said the room is the same size as before. I kind of agree with him because pallets are about four or five feet square, and someone would need a lot of space to hide those pallets."

"If the artifacts are still on the pallets."

"I agree. But there were a lot of boxes on those pallets."

"Well, they are somewhere. Anything else you find while I was chugging away on paperwork?"

"Probably nothing you don't already know. I checked public files on court cases, probate, land records, and corporation filings. Nothing on Jerome Hemmingway."

"No surprise there."

"Another elusive fellow Steven Salinas. Made lots of money, invested lots of money, left no footprints."

"That's not the case with Kagoona. Everyone knows of Henry. And if you did not know of him, he'd tell you."

Noonan chuckled. "I've got a few more places to look. I'll get around to it after we talk with Harrison Anderson."

"Well buckle up, Buttercup. He was not in a good mood when he left the message on my answering machine."

CHAPTER 44

Harrison Anderson was, to parrot an expression Noonan had heard from California recruits during his stint in the United States Army, "not a happy camper."

But it was also clear Harrison Anderson did not have a leg to stand on: legally, ethically or morally. He knew it. Bernice Whitcomb knew it. Heinz Noonan knew it. But Whitcomb and Noonan knew a discussion was necessary. That was the way of the world.

But it also told Noonan he and Whitcomb were very close to the truth. Noonan was still in the dark as to where the artifacts were secreted and even more important, why anyone would steal something that had no value.

Anderson was restrained because he had no choice. "I keep getting complaints from people around town," he said as he casually eyed Whitcomb and Noonan across the top of his littered desk. "You two are pulling people away from their regular jobs, creating problems up their administrative food chain."

Whitcomb was politically polite. "Well, I, we, understand that. But, you see, there is still the matter of the missing artifacts. My company is on the hook for that loss. At the present time we do not have a clue where the artifacts are, and I have not received a peep from the perpetrators."

"Sorry?" Anderson was taken by surprise.

182

"Mr. Anderson, you live in a clean world. I do not. Many times, when a theft occurs, the insurance company is approached by the perpetrators. They, the perpetrators, suggest that if the insurance company pays them, say, 15% of the value of the theft, the perpetrators will return the stolen items. The insurance company then has a choice: pay 15% to disreputable individuals or 100% to the victims."

"So, you pay?" Anderson was shocked. "Is that legal?"

"As far as I know, no one has gone to jail to recover stolen items at 15% of face value."

"That's, that's, that's, hard to believe."

"If you are not in the industry, I understand. But, as far as we are concerned," Whitcomb pointed to herself and Noonan, "we have an open case of theft. Captain Noonan has offered his services at no cost, and I cannot say no to having a person with his experience on the case. My company is on the hook for the replacement value of those artifacts, and I have people from the home office who are on the phone every day asking me what's happening. And every day I say the same thing: 'I'm working on it.'"

Anderson seemed to lose steam. "I do understand, Ms Whitcomb, but I get calls every day from people who you and the captain have interviewed. They are not happy. Is this going to continue?"

Noonan cut in. "That's a good question and one with no answer. Investigations continue where they are leads. We have followed a large number of leads that have gone nowhere. There are still some leads to follow so the quick answer to your question is I, we," he pointed at Whitcomb, "do not know. But until the artifacts are found, we have to keep looking."

Anderson knew when he was beaten. "Well, do it quickly. I do not like getting call after call from people who have been subjected to the nth degree. Captain, you will leave Anchorage, but I have to stay here."

Noonan played his political card. "I understand, Mr. Anderson. I will be leaving in about three days so, win or lose, my part of this investigation will be wrapped up by then. After that, Ms Whitcomb and her company are on the hook for the value of the artifacts."

Anderson gave an imperial wave of his hand to indicate the meeting was at an end.

CHAPTER 45

In snow country, from Alaska to Maine and across the northern tier of states, there is a time frame known as 'breakup.' Unknown to the southern tier of states like Arizona, New Mexico, Texas and the Deep South, breakup occurs when the temperature of the earth rises high enough to melt the snow and ice that has been on the ground since the start of winter. That's December 21st in the Lower 48 states but, in Alaska, about September 15th.

Breakup in Alaska is a celebrated event because it means the land is picking up about five more minutes of sunlight every day. The more sunlight there is, the more snow melts. But there is a downside, particularly in the bush, that area of Alaska that is unreachable by road. Those villages depend on an airplane for their food and supplies and, once a year, barges that plow their way up the rivers with cargo too heavy for airplanes. But barges cannot get up the river until all the ice on the rivers has broken apart and been swept out to the sea. When the river breaks, it is clogged with riverbergs, many of them the size of buildings. Ice jams are frequent, and it is not unusual for a village to be quickly flooded if there is an ice jam nearby.

There are no ice jams in Sandersonville or, for that matter, in North Carolina. But Noonan was married to an Alaskan, so he used the term frequently. Whitcomb lived in Alaska and had no trouble using the term.

"We've got an ice jam here," Noonan said as he and Whitcomb left Anderson's office. "We are close to finished."

"How do you know that?"

"Simple. Three things. First, Anderson is worried. Second, we know where the artifacts are."

This took Whitcomb by surprise. "How's that? Or, rather, why?"

"There is only one place the artifacts can be. At the Municipal Hospital."

"How'd you figure that out?"

"Everything, every clue leads back to the hospital, not the Anchorage Warehouse and Storage Facility. Where I do not know. Yet. But I am convinced the artifacts are in the hospital. I'm betting the boxes and crates were taken off the pallets in the Chugach Shipping garage and taken to the Hospital in small loads. Then they were hidden someplace in the hospital."

Whitcomb shook her head like a cartoon character who had just been told an unbelievable excuse. "What am I missing? Why steal the artifacts in the first place?"

"That, Ms Whitcomb, I don't know. Not yet. But it has something to do with money. How, I do not know. But some people have gone to an extreme length to make those artifacts disappear."

"OK, I'll bite. Why?"

"We have to follow the money. Right now, I see no money angle. But there is a money angle. When we find it, we find the perpetrators."

"Then what do we do?"

"If I knew that, Bernice, I could make a fortune as a psychic."

CHAPTER 46

The next day, the ice broke. It didn't cause an ice jam, but it started events tumbling. It was not until the evening that Noonan had a chance to get back onto the internet in his hotel room to look for clues. Kagoona had run for State Senate and Noonan had been advised to look at Kagoona's campaign filings. Since Noonan had never run for office, he had no idea what kind of documents and records were needed. It was too late to ask anyone, so he just went to the State of Alaska website and punched in 'elections.' That took him to the Alaska Public Offices Commission, and he found a tab for 'public documents.' When he hit that tab, he had a spread of document files.

Since he was looking for a money angle, he started with campaign donations for Kagoona. There were tens of thousands of dollars in donations, many in small amounts. Name by name, Noonan went down the list. Several of the names he recognized: Johnathan Hemmingway, Regina Hemmingway, Steven Salinas, and Elmore McCommon. All of these donations were several hundred dollars apiece, in the middle range amount of the rest of the donations. Nothing jumped out at him.

Noonan then saw a link for POFD/LFD. What was that? So, he pulled it up. POFD stood for Public Official Financial Disclosure and LFD stood for Legislative Financial Disclosure. Since Kagoona had not been elected, the LFD would not have a file on Kagoona. But there was one on him in the POFD. The POFD was a barebones look at the financial status of the candidate. Kagoona had an impressive list of assets and income but nothing specific. This was because the values were in degrees, as in 'between $1,000 and $25,000,' rather than actual amounts. The report was generic, boring, and lacking in specificity.

Except for one item.

Kagoona was listed as a shareholder – without a dollar value attached – of Yukon Ltd. in Denver.

Denver?

That was odd.

A distant gong sounded in Noonan's cerebellum.

So, he pulled up the list of corporations for Colorado. It took a while because Colorado had a lot more people than Alaska, so it took a while to weave his way to the officers of the corporation. It was based out of a Post Office Box in Denver. No surprise there. But what was a surprise were the officers:

Henry Kagoona, President
Steven Salinas, Vice President
Harrison Anderson, Secretary
Johnathan Hemmingway, Treasurer
Elmore McCommon, Board member
BINGO!

The money angle at last!

Maybe.

But there was a problem.

You do not form a corporation if there is no money coming in. So where was the money coming in?

Even more important, there were two names missing. Jerome Hemmingway was not listed and this, Noonan mused, was par for the course. Jerome Hemmingway could not be part of the corporation because he was in the Senior Home for Pioneers. To be admitted you had to give up your assets to the State of Alaska. Besides, at his age and in the Senior Home for Pioneers, he didn't need any money.

But Noonan was surprised to see that Regina Hemmingway was not listed as a member of the corporation. That could only mean one thing: she was not part of the cabal. But she was being used. She was not going to be happy about that.

Excited, Noonan then 'followed the money.' You form a corporation to make money. Money had to come in. Where that money was coming from Noonan did not know. Where was it going? Logically, since the corporation was in Colorado, the money would be invested in Colorado. Since the corporation had Jerome Hemmingway's fingerprints and he was an estate *guru,* the money would probably be invested in land. This was reasonable because if the corporation received money, it had to pay income taxes. The best way to avoid paying income taxes was to buy things to drive up the expenses which were tax deductions. If the money coming in was big, which it had to be to form a corporation, the expenses had to be large as well.

The date of the formation of the corporation was about the same time as the formation of the Aboriginal Artifact Commission and when the National Bank of Anchorage Museum was collapsing. That might be a clue, but Noonan would have to follow that lead later. But right now, at midnight in Anchorage, he was hot the trail he understood best: money.

The most logical place to hide large amounts of money in new corporations was land. So, Noonan wandered the State of Colorado URL until he found land title searches. This was not as easy as it seemed because the titles were scattered by county. To start with. But he had the names of the Board members, so he waded into the land record swamp. It took almost an hour for him to find a piece of property listed as owned by Elmore McCommon. It was a $200,000 share of a building in Pueblo.

But there was something very odd about the purchase. It had been made three weeks earlier. Then, a week later, the share had been transferred to a trust, the Kuskokwim Trust. Noonan then went to the listings of trusts filed in Colorado. The Kuskokwim Trust had been legally formed a week *before* McCommon's property had been transferred to the trust. It was a classical money laundering operation. You take the money coming in – in this case cash from some source – and then legally hide it by buying property. Then, to keep it from being legally seized, you hide it in a trust. That way you cannot lose it in a lawsuit. When Noonan pulled up the names of the people in the trust, they matched the names of the men in Yukon, Ltd.

Noonan now had one-third of the answer to why the artifacts had been hidden. It was not for the value of the artifacts, it was to hide the transfer of money *to* Yukon, Ltd. Where the money originally came from was unknown to Noonan at this time. The second third of the scam was to keep from paying taxes on the money coming in. So, the money was used to buy land, a legitimate business expenditure. If enough land was purchased, which Noonan believed to be the case, all the money coming in would be invested in land and, as there was no cash left, there were no income taxes due. Third, by transferring the land into a trust, the money would be safe from a lawsuit. If someone wanted to sue for the return of the money, they would have to sue Yukon, Ltd. first. But even if they won, Yukon, Ltd. did not have the property. Kuskokwim, Inc. did. So, the lawsuit would have to proceed against Kuskokwim, Inc. Noonan knew from experience that assets in trusts cannot be attached if they have been in the trust for at least 18 months. So, if the lawsuit against Yukon, Ltd. and Kuskokwim, Inc. lasted longer than 18 months, there would be no money to attach legally. Jerome Hemingway's fingerprints were all over this scam.

But the discovery of the trust cleared up one puzzling question: why had the artifacts been stolen? The answer: give the 18-month clock as much ticking time as possible. When the alarm bell rang 18 months and one second after the formation of the Kuskokwim Trust, the five Board members of Yukon, Inc. could sell the investments and pocket the cash.

And there might not be a way to stop them.

CHAPTER 47

"No way!"

"Way!"

"Really? You found all of that while I was asleep? Hey, you are worth every penny I am paying you!" Whitcomb reached across the table at the Alascattalo Café and Bar and punched Noonan on his shoulder. "Kudos to you!"

"Actually, it was easy. Once you are on the right track, everything falls into place. Well, almost everything."

"Well, now we know where the money is going. But it is already 'there,' so to speak. So where did it come from? And what does it have to do with the missing artifacts?"

Noonan swirled the coffee in his cup. "I am pretty sure the artifacts are in the hospital. I want another look inside the basement. Rather, the ground floor of the western entrance. And I don't want any interference. That's why we're meeting here and not at your office."

"Why are we meeting here?"

"You are the only person the bad people can follow. I'm in a hotel. Johnathan is keeping an eye on his sister."

"You don't think she's involved?"

"Nothing says she is. Everything says she's being kept in the dark by her brother. If I were on the other team, so to speak, I'd be following you. As long as you are far away from the hospital, the artifacts are safe. Now, as was constantly said on Black Adder, 'I have a devious plan.'"

"Whenever that was said, the plan didn't work."

"Yes, but this is not a television sitcom. First, I need you to make me a chicken sandwich."

CHAPTER 48

"You!"

Noonan held his hands out wide. "I know. I lied. I'm a horrible guy. I know me well but what can I say?" He held out the chicken sandwich. "But I did not come alone!"

"At least you came with an offering. I'm afraid to ask, why are you here?"

"I need a name."

"Barak Obama." Sylvester Flynn smiled as he reached for the chicken sandwich.

"Not that one." Noonan handed Flynn the sandwich. "I need the name of someone who can let me into the locked area behind the elevator shafts at the western entrance."

"Sure, Elmore McCommon."

"No, not Elmore. Someone else."

"Well, it can't be done at night."

"I want it done during the day."

"Give me your phone number and I will see what I can do."

"All I need to do is know a few hours ahead of time."

"I'm sure that someone will want a chicken sandwich. I'll see what I can do."

CHAPTER 49

"Look, I'm not one of those women who whines and complains about being treated badly with no cause. And I don't work with Elmore McCommon but let me make it clear. I am investigating a crime. I am not a cop, but I can get the cops here. And this crime involves millions. The response I got from McCommon when I wanted to see inside the downstairs rooms was the equivalent of 'Get the whippy-do out of here, b…

The Equity Officer at the Anchorage Municipal Hospital, Maria Jose Hernandez was taking notes. She had a blank look on her face, a traditional bureaucratic expression.

"I don't want to cause problems for you or the hospital. And I don't want to call the police because then there'll be a police report. What I was hoping you would do is call Mr. McCommon in here, *right now*, while I am here, and make it clear to him, with me here, I am to be given access to the downstairs rooms We can set up a time so it will not interfere with his schedule. I'm not unfeeling. But I need to set up a time that is convenient for him. And me."

Maria Jose Hernandez reached for the phone on her desk.

CHAPTER 50

At the same moment, Noonan handed the chicken sandwich to a woman who would not give her name. That was fine with Noonan. He just wanted to look into the rooms on the mezzanine floor of the western entrance. The unnamed woman tapped a code into the door beside the elevator shaft.

"Please do not take very long. I don't want any trouble," she said as she swung the door open.

From the open door, Noonan could see McCommon's office was empty. He pointed to the doors in the back of the alcove. One at a time the unnamed woman opened the doors. Two of them were abandoned offices, the third was jampacked with wheelchairs, some ladders and lounge chairs and walkers. As Noonan looked inside, the woman stood outside of the room and munched on her chicken sandwich.

"That's it."

"How about those doors," Noonan pointed to the doors at the back of the elevator shafts.

"Those require a passcode I don't have. They're only opened when there is trouble with the elevators." She jerked her head toward McCommon's office. "Elmore McCommon is in charge of that. Other than a yearly checkup, you know the old saying, 'If it ain't broke don't fix it.'"

Another gong went off in Noonan's cerebral cavity.

CHAPTER 51

When Choi Walton at the National Bank of Anchorage saw Noonan and Whitcomb, she had the same reaction as someone seeing a corpse rise from a grave in a cemetery on a moonless night at midnight. Noonan and Whitcomb did not bother to ask if they could sit down. They just sat. Noonan pulled out a notebook for show and from the look on Walton's face, it had its effect.

"Now, Ms Walton," Noonan said slowly and methodically, "the last time we talked, you said you could tell me about the bank accounts of William Chambers because they were in probate. Is that correct?"

Walton stumbled through something that sounded like a positive response.

"Well, let's see, at that time there were three. Two of them were closed. The third one was still open and held about $5,000."

Again, the extended verbal stumble.

"We," Noonan pointed to Whitcomb as he spoke, "would like to know how much is in that account now."

This time the verbal stumble was extensive. But it finished with the inevitable, "I would have to check with my supervisor to see if I can release that information."

Noonan kind of looked around the room – for show – until he saw the security camera on the wall behind Walton's desk. Walton's bodily action made it clear she had seen Noonan see the security camera. Then Noonan gave just enough time to appear casual and looked back to Walton. Softly he said, "There is no reason for the National Bank of Anchorage (he paused for effect) or you to get dragged into a police investigation. I know you have your responsibilities here. But that account is part of the probate. Tell you what, me and my partner," Noonan tilted his head toward Whitcomb, "will be at the Alascattalo Café and Grill in an hour. If you were to show up and have a cup of coffee, you might find us there by accident and engage in a pleasant conversation. We," again the nod toward Whitcomb, "don't want to cause you or the National Bank of Anchorage any bad publicity by getting a court order."

Walton's face matched the pale wall of her office.

CHAPTER 52

"Ten million."

This took both Noonan and Whitcomb by surprise.

"Ten million?" Noonan asked as he wrote the figure in his notebook. "Ten million came in?"

"And out," Walton said as she sipped her coffee. She gave a nervous look around the coffee bar.

"We're alone," Whitcomb told her. "We're meeting here rather than in my office because we wanted a quiet conversation. Now, ten million dollars went into the account of William Chambers after he died, correct?"

"Oh, yes. It was startling. Then it went out an hour later."

"Where did it go?" Noonan asked.

"To the account of the nonprofit that tried to raise money to save the museum."

Whitcomb leaned forward and asked, "Are you sure? I thought that nonprofit was dead."

Walton looked around nervously. "I did too. But Harrison Anderson showed up to get the check from the Chambers account. He said it was to go to the nonprofit. He had a copy of the notarized nonprofit filing from the State of Alaska and a notarized vote, I guess you'd call it, from the nonprofit board authorizing the transfer of funds. I had my supervisor OK the transfer. I'm sure she called the men who signed the notarized vote. I don't see just accepting the paperwork at face value."

Noonan was intent on his next question. "Whose names were on the notarized vote?"

"Three. There was Jerome and Johnathan Hemmingway. I'm aware of them. Harrison Anderson was the third signature and I had him verify his identity with his driver's license. After I got the OK to give him the check, he opened a new account in the name of the nonprofit. Then he deposited the money from the Chambers account to the non-profit account.

"Just like that?" Whitcomb said. "Just opened a new account and put in $10 million?"

"Yeah. Then the money was transferred to a corporation out of state. I can't legally tell you how much money is left in that account now, but you could not buy this cup of coffee," she raised her paper cup of latte, "with what was left."

CHAPTER 53

Choi Walton left the Alascattalo Café and Bar like a human cannonball.

"What is going on?" Whitcomb was still stunned. "What did we just hear?"

Noonan smiled. "The oldest game on earth, getting money and hiding it so no one knows how much you have. Or where it is. Here's what I figure happened. The National Bank of Anchorage Museum was way more than a museum. It was a way for the Chambers family to run up phony expenses. They probably claimed all kinds of deductions using the museum as an umbrella."

"Like what?"

"Oh, they could say the six family members spent 15 hours a month donating time to the museum even though none of them had ever come to Alaska. Then they'd claim office business expenses, travel and entertainment, depreciation in their homes. I'm sure Jerome Hemmingway was advising them. Whatever they did, it was legal. Devious but legal. The museum was a cash cow in the sense they could use their phony expenses to reduce their income tax burden."

"M-a-y-b-e," Whitcomb was confused. "But ten million is a lot of money for a museum that isn't worth anything."

"Yes and no. Yes, the museum is not worth ten million if you sell the artifacts on the street, but the assessed value could be that high. Probably is. I'm not an accountant but I figure the Chambers family was contacted by Jerome Hemmingway when William dying. He said he could show, on paper, how much the museum was worth."

Whitcomb started to talk but Noonan cut her off. "Not how much the artifacts altogether were *worth* but their *assessed* value. How much it would cost to *replace* the artifacts. That would be expensive. Ten million dollars expensive. He likely said he could justify, on paper, ten million dollars. The family was probably pleased as punch because donations to a nonprofit are tax deductions. I don't know how much William Chambers was worth but ten million would go a long way in reducing any taxes. If inheritances are taxed, I'm not sure. But I am sure the ten million spent was a benefit to the family. It was a ten-million-dollar write-off. That might be peanuts to them but to our five conspirators, it was, quite literally, money in the bank."

"And legal?"

"Probably. If and when the IRS ever shows up, it will want to see paperwork supporting the ten-million-dollar figure. Legally, and I'm sure the paperwork is there, ownership of the Chambers Museum was transferred to the nonprofit. The nonprofit was never disbanded so, technically and legally, it still owns all of the artifacts. So, there are records to prove the nonprofit had ten million dollars of assets. All the nonprofit needed to do to make the transfer of the $10 million legal was to get the Board of Directors to agree to the transfer. This was all done in advance. Please note that Regina Hemmingway's name is not on the transfer. She gets nothing so that pretty much clears her of any culpability with this scam. By the time the IRS does catch up to the three, Jerome will be dead. They've been planning this for three years so there would be no slip ups. From what I can see, there are no loose ends."

"Will the nonprofit have that paperwork?"

"I'm sure it does. Jerome Hemmingway was no slouch. The IRS might whine and moan, but the nonprofit is gone. Its assets were legally transferred to Yukon, Ltd. So, the money from the nonprofit has been legally washed, laundered. By the time the IRS does get around to investigating, if it ever does, the money will be long gone. Then, even if the IRS is diligent, it will take years to pierce the corporate veil of Yukon, Ltd. and then the Kuskokwim Trust. Anyone suing will only have 18 months to get any money because after that, the money is in trust is inviolate."

"Maybe."

Noonan smiled. "Now you're thinking like a cop. We don't have a good grip on where the books of the Chambers Museum are. They would have been transferred to the nonprofit. Those records would be proof the nonprofit had legitimate assets and the transfer was not just a money laundering scheme. As long as the money stays in trust for 18 months, it's free and clear."

"Except if fraud is involved."

"True. But there is no fraud here. Sleazy, yes. Fraud, no."

Whitcomb shook her head. "What if the Chambers Museum records are never found?"

Noonan smiled and he, too, shook his head. "If the Chambers Museum records and the nonprofit books are not with the artifacts when they are found, the IRS is going to have to take the word of the original appraisal by Jerome Hemmingway at face value. He will probably be dead by that time. This was not Jerome Hemmingway's first rodeo."

"Probably his last."

"I agree," Noonan said as he shook his head. "And for the five men in the Kuskokwim Corporation it is nothing but winner, winner, chicken dinner."

"So, here we are at the end of the road. How did you figure out where the artifacts were hidden?"

"Only place they could be. The hospital was a perfect hiding place. The new elevator shaft at the hospital was only going to service people from the eastern entrance. For them, that means the ground floor. On the eastern side of the hospital. But the elevator shaft had to go all the way down to the western entrance for stability. That's where the motor and cables were located. But that left about 30 feet of empty space, unused space. So, the artifact boxes were most likely taken off the pallets and, one at a time, were moved into the empty space in the new elevator shaft. Johnathan and the Kagoona twins would arrive, meet with McCommon, and have him open the secure elevator door. There was so much activity in the construction site that a couple of men moving boxes on dollies would not be suspicious."

"Then why remove the stairs?"

"My guess is some of the crates were too big to be moved by a hand dolly. The solution was to move the crates on a flatbed. I'm also betting they needed time to maneuver the crates into the elevator shaft. By removing the stairs, there was an excuse for Chugach Shipping to bring in new ones. No one wanted to take the blame for the stairs being missing so everyone just turned a blind eye when Chugach Shipping brought in the new stairs. When the Chugach Shipping people went behind the wall – if anyone cared – the excuse would be to bolt the missing stairs in the back of the wall. Even if someone had seen the men with the flatbeds during the day, the excuse would have been that you have to behind the wall to bolt the new stairs in place. Apparently, it worked because no one said Butkus about the missing stairs or their reattachment. After the large crates were maneuvered into the elevator shaft, the new stairs were reattached and away went Chugach Shipping. Even if someone had seen them behind the wall, they had an excuse.

"My bet, the largest crates came at night. They were probably have attracted attention if they had been brought in during the day. When the large crates, one or several, were brought in at night, Elmore McCommon wiped the security tapes clean the next morning."

Whitcomb put her coffee down with a vengeance. "So, at the end of the day, the bad people get away with it."

Noonan shook his head. "The cleverest criminals never get caught. My bet, William Chambers and his family knew he was on his way out. Jerome had set up the National Bank of Anchorage Museum and the initial tax scam, so he was asked to come up with a Plan B. Or Jerome knew William Chambers was dying. Either way, it didn't matter. Everyone involved had time, so they established the Aboriginal Artifact Commission. I'm sure Jerome Hemmingway knew Harrison Anderson from Fairbanks. Probably Henry Kagoona too. He knew they were morally adjustable. Steven Salinas too. Jerome Hemmingway had adopted Regina and Johnathan, so he knew Johnathan was morally adjustable. Regina was not. That's why she's not a party to any of the shenanigans. McCommon was needed because he had the access to the elevator shafts and could keep the artifacts under wraps as long as possible."

"Why did Jerome need the Aboriginal Artifact Commission if he also had the nonprofit?"

"Cover. He also needed an entity to hide the artifacts and validate the inflated replacement cost. That had to be done by the Aboriginal Artifact Commission so there was, what is called in legal circles, an 'arm's length' transaction. On paper, there was no *reasonable, legal* link between the replacement assessment and the Aboriginal Artifact Commission. It also gave the cabal time to set the entire scheme in motion. This was not a case of taking advantage of a sudden opportunity. It was well-planned and well-executed. From the looting of the artifacts to the switching of delivery paperwork by Steven Salinas in the warehouse. A box at a time, the artifacts were hidden in the Municipal Hospital. Then six pallets of some other material were sent to the Anchorage Warehouse with the artifact paperwork. That was proof the artifacts had made it to the warehouse. Then the paperwork was switched in the records room. Poof, the artifacts were gone on paper. All done with precision because of the planning. It worked like a charm."

"And legal," snapped Whitcomb.

"Yup," replied Noonan. "In California, the expression is zip. We've got zip. No illegal activity has occurred. The artifacts will be 'found,'" Noonan made quote marks in the air with his index fingers, "and every-one will be DKN."

"DKN?"

"Don't Know Nothing. There will be no artifacts missing and if there ever is a police report it will say it was just a mix up, end of story. Your company is now off the hook for any damages. I will go back to North Carolina with a case closed and Regina Hemmingway will ..."

"Regina? How does she benefit?"

"She's got a crook for a brother. He's been conning her for years. I think she believes she's been stuck with him because, well, he's her brother. I mean, she's doing all the work and all he is doing is managing truck deliveries. Once you tell her what has gone down ..."

"I'm going to tell her?"

"Absolutely. Sometimes a woman-to-woman conversation is the best way to handle a delicate situation. You can also tell her that the truth is going to get out. James Hayworth at the newspaper is following this story. Legally, there is nothing anyone can do. But the press is not bound to keep the matter quiet. Tell Regina that the story is going to come out and it would be better if her brother were gone."

"He'll fight her."

"He can't. He's an employee. He doesn't have a share of the company. She can just fire him. If he does fight, she can tell him she thinks he committed fraud. And she has the delivery records to link him to the artifacts. Besides, he's walking away with two million dollars in property."

"Yeah, but that leaves Regina without someone running the operation downstairs. The trucks and warehouse."

"Nope. There's Lael Morgan. She's one smart cookie. A bit off on socialism but give her a taste of capitalism and I'm sure she'll change her tune."

"How is Hayworth going to find out about the recovery of the artifacts?"

"You're going to tell him. You always want to get out ahead of a story. Makes you look better that way."

"Why do I want to look better?"

"To keep Regina in the clear. She doesn't deserve the bad publicity. After all, by the time the story comes out, Johnathan will no longer be with Chugach Shipping. With luck, he'll be in Pueblo watching his property."

"What about the Aboriginal Artifact Commission?"

"It's going, going, gone. I'm sure it was set up as a front for the artifact scam. The money has washed through the Commission. The artifacts will have been found and distributed. I'm sure Harrison Anderson will hold a press conference and say that the work of the Commission is done. It has been a success. All of the artifacts from the National Bank of Anchorage Museum have been distributed and the Commission is closing its doors."

"And Jerome is going to be gone soon," Whitcomb said with a faux sigh, "leaving Regina the only one in town."

"You got it. And there will be no one in town to tell the tale. Rack one up for the bad boys."

"What about you?"

"I'll be on the beach on the Outer Banks of North Carolina leaving this mess to you! However," he paused. "I need you to do one more thing for me."

"Which is?"

"I need one more chicken sandwich."

CHAPTER 54

If Jerome Hemmingway was surprised to see Noonan, he didn't show it. But then again, he was a consummate actor.

"Do I know you?"

"Not really," Noonan said as he handed him a chicken sandwich. "I'm on my way out of town and I wanted to personally deliver a chicken sandwich."

Hemmingway fell out of character for a nanosecond and then recovered. "Chicken sandwich. How nice. Do I know you?"

"Nope. I'm not an Alaskan and I'm going home to North Carolina. I just wanted to gloat for an instant. To use a North Carolina saying, I'm going home a winner, winner, chicken dinner. I thought you deserved at least a part of that dinner."

"How nice. What for? Do I know you?"

Noonan pointed to the chicken sandwich. "Do you know why the police investigate eggs being stolen from the coup?"

Hemmingway said nothing but his eyes said it all.

"Fowl play."

CHAPTER 55

I'll bet you had a tough time in Alaska," said Harriet, the Sandersonville Police Department office manager and common-sense maven. "I mean, it got all the way up to, ooohhh, what 75 with a humidity of zero?"

"Yes," Noonan replied without looking up from a cold case file. "It was terrible. In-laws from morning till night. Tough, tough. I was like bread on vacation.

"Sorry."

"I loafed."